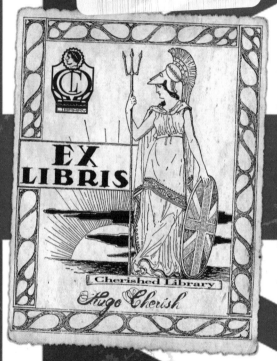

EX
LIBRIS

Cherished Library

Hugo Cherish

Great
Britons

A Very Peculiar History™

With added stiff upper lip

Grrr!

'The Britons are quite separated from
all the world.'

Virgil,
classical Roman poet.

To Alex

IG

Editor: Victoria England

Artists: David Antram, Mark Bergin, Penko Gelev, Nick Hewetson, John James, Sarah Kensington, Mark Peppé, Carolyn Scrace, Gerald Wood

Published in Great Britain in MMXI by
Book House, an imprint of
The Salariya Book Company Ltd
25 Marlborough Place, Brighton BN1 1UB
www.salariya.com
www.book-house.co.uk

HB ISBN-13: 978-1-907184-59-8

1 3 5 7 9 8 6 4 2
A CIP catalogue record for this book is available
from the British Library.
Printed and bound in Dubai.
Printed on paper from sustainable sources.

Visit our website at **www.book-house.co.uk**
or go to **www.salariya.com**
for **free** electronic versions of:
You Wouldn't Want to be an Egyptian Mummy!
You Wouldn't Want to be a Roman Gladiator!
You Wouldnt Want to Join Shackleton's Polar Expedition!
You Wouldn't Want to Sail on a 19th-Century Whaling Ship!

'I know I have the body but of a weak and feeble woman, but I have the heart and stomach of a king, and a King of England too...'

Queen Elizabeth I, addressing her troops at Tilbury, at the time of the attack on England by the Spanish Armada in 1588.

'The English are not happy unless they are miserable, the Irish are not at peace unless they are at war, and the Scots are not at home unless they are abroad.'

George Orwell

'If the British Empire and its Commonwealth last for a thousand years, men will still say, *this* was their finest hour.'

British Prime Minister, Winston Churchill, in a speech he made in 1940 to prepare the British people for the great struggle that was expected when Nazi Germany defeated France and turned its full might against Britain.

Great Britons

A Very Peculiar History™

With added stiff upper lip

Written by
Ian Graham

Created and designed by
David Salariya

Contents

Britons and Britain: 10 fascinating facts

1. Britons are the natives and inhabitants of the island of Great Britain from ancient times.

2. Great Britain is the biggest island in Europe and the ninth biggest in the world.

3. Before the Romans invaded Britain in AD 43, Britain was a patchwork of different tribes, groups and cultures.

4. The Romans called the part of the island that they controlled (everything south of Scotland) Britannia.

5. Today, Great Britain is a single nation consisting of England, Wales and Scotland, but it did not exist until 1707, when England and Wales were united with Scotland. It forms part of the United Kingdom of Great Britain and Northern Ireland.

6. The highest point in Britain is the top of Ben Nevis: a 1,344-metre (4,409-ft) tall mountain in Scotland. The lowest point is in The Fens in eastern England, which are 4 metres (13.1 ft) below sea level.

7. The scale and spread of the British Empire ensured that English would become the leading language of business and science around the world. Up to 400 million people speak English as their first language and another billion or so speak English as their second language.

8. The population of Great Britain (England, Scotland and Wales) is approximately 60 million.

9. Between the 16th century and the middle of the 20th century, Britain established an empire that was the biggest in history. At its height, it encompassed a quarter of the world's population and a quarter of the world's total land area. Most of Britain's former colonies, dominions and territories are now independent countries.

10. Britain's longest river, also the biggest in terms of water flow, is the Severn. From its source in the Cambrian Mountains in Wales to its end in the Bristol Channel it measures 354 km (220 miles) in length.

Putting Britons on the map

Famous and important Britons and their places of birth in Great Britain.

1. **Elton John** – born in Middlesex, 1947
2. **Beatrix Potter** – born in Kensington, 1866
3. **Alexander Graham Bell** – born in Edinburgh, 1847
4. **Captain James Cook** – born in Yorkshire, 1728
5. **Gustav Holst** – born in Cheltenham, 1874
6. **Charles Dickens** – born in Portsmouth, 1812
7. **Fred Perry** – born in Stockport, 1909
8. **Dame Julie Andrews** – born in Surrey, 1935
9. **David Hockney** – born in Bradford, 1937
10. **Sir Christopher Wren** – born in Wiltshire, 1632
11. **Sir Isaac Newton** – born in Lincolnshire, 1643
12. **Emmeline Pankhurst** – born in Manchester, 1858
13. **Charles Darwin** – born in Shropshire, 1809
14. **Jane Austen** – born in Hampshire, 1775
15. **Dick Turpin** – born in Essex, 1705

'If you lead a country like Britain, a strong country which has taken lead in world affairs in good times and in bad, a country that is always reliable, then you have to have a touch of iron about you.'

British Prime Minister Margaret Thatcher

'In the end it may well be that Britain will be honoured by historians more for the way she disposed of an empire than for the way in which she acquired it.'

Lord Harlech

'England is a nation of shopkeepers.'

Napoleon Bonaparte

'Rule Britannia! Britannia rule the waves; Britons never will be slaves.'

James Thompson

INTRODUCTION

History is peppered with Britons who have shown great leadership, an adventurous spirit, astonishing courage or brilliant creativity in science, medicine, engineering and the arts. It is impossible to include all of them in this book. The scientists, engineers, politicians, military leaders, kings and queens, entertainers, sports men and women, adventurers and others that have been featured are a personal selection of the many that could have been included.

An island nation

As an island nation, Britain has always looked outwards to the rest of the world. Many of the greatest Britons made their mark on the wider world, not just within Britain.

For centuries, Britain's military power and its ability to defend itself depended on its navy. Generations of naval training produced seamen who not only protected the nation but also explored the rest of the world.

Britain's naval power also enabled it to establish the biggest empire the world has ever seen. It was said that the *'sun never sets on the British Empire'*, because British colonies and territories were spread around the whole world. On old maps, they are the parts of the world coloured pink. During the twentieth century, the days of empire ended. It was no longer acceptable for great powers to rule other countries that were claimed and conquered in a past age. Britain's former colonies were granted independence. As a result, Britain is no longer one of the world's superpowers.

Industrial Revolution

Most revolutions are violent events with a great deal of death and destruction, but one of the most important revolutions in history began in Britain during the eighteenth century without armies clashing or revolutionaries storming the capital. It was the industrial revolution. The invention of the steam engine in 1712 by Thomas Newcomen gave industry a reliable source of power for its machines that did not depend on wind or water. By the middle of the nineteenth century, Britain was the world's leading industrial power. The first modern factories were built at this time. People began moving off the land and into cities to work in the new factories. The industrial revolution and the inventions it spawned transformed the whole world. The newly invented railways enabled people and goods to travel further and faster than ever before.

War and conflict

Britain and its military forces have been involved in dozens of wars at home and abroad. These conflicts have produced some exceptional national and military leaders and heroes. Two world wars also harnessed the genius of British scientists and inventors, who created new technologies, including the jet engine and electronic computers.

Invention

Britain has a great tradition of science, engineering and invention. British scientists including Robert Hooke and Sir Isaac Newton were at the forefront of unravelling the secrets of the universe. British doctors and scientists made important discoveries in medicine, including penicillin and the structure of DNA.

British engineers and inventors gave the world some of the most important inventions ever made, including the steam engine, railways, the telephone and television.

Kings and queens

Britain is a democratic nation run by a government elected by the people, but it is also a monarchy. Today, the monarchy is largely ceremonial. Kings and queens have ruled the British people in an almost unbroken line for more than a thousand years.

Honorary great Britons

One of the most famous Britons – St George, the patron saint of England – wasn't British at all! He is thought to have been born in Cappadocia, in Turkey today, and then moved to Palestine. He became a Roman soldier in the Emperor Diocletian's army. In AD 303, he protested against the emperor's persecution of Christians and was executed at Lydda in Palestine. In legend, he is supposed to have slain a dragon, but this is a medieval invention. He was claimed as patron saint by England (and many other countries).

Several other important figures in British history were born elsewhere but made Britain their home. Anthony van Dyck (1599–1641) was a Flemish artist. He became the official court painter to King Charles I in 1623. He was granted some rights of citizenship, paid a pension and given a house by the king. He also married a lady-in-waiting to the queen.

Other honorary great Britons include George Frideric Handel (1685–1759), who spent half of his life in Britain composing music for King George I and his successor, George II. Karl Marx (1818–1883), a Prussian philosopher, lived in London from 1849 until his death. His ideas and writings contributed to the development of communism. Prince Albert of Saxe-Coburg and Gotha (1819–1861), the husband of Queen Victoria, was born near Coburg, Germany. Albert, who was also Victoria's cousin, led reforms in education, social welfare and slavery in Britain. He also took a great interest in the application of science to industry. He was responsible for the modern idea that the royal family should be separate from and above politics.

fictional great Britons

Some Britons who are celebrated for their adventures and achievements never existed! Writers and film-makers have created and popularised many fictional British characters including King Arthur, Sherlock Holmes, Biggles, James Bond and Robin Hood.

King Arthur
The legend of King Arthur dates back more than a thousand years. Arthur's right to the throne was established when he pulled a sword from a stone – something that could only be done by the true king. He is said to have lived in a castle called Camelot with his wife, Guinevere, and the Knights of the Round Table. The most famous knights were Sir Lancelot and Sir Galahad. Arthur was armed with a magical sword called Excalibur, which was given to him by a mysterious *'Lady of the Lake'*. He was assisted by a wizard called Merlin.

James 'Biggles' Bigglesworth

Biggles was a pilot and gentleman adventurer who featured in nearly 100 books written by W.E Johns (1893–1968). Biggles, like Johns, was a World War I pilot. He also went on to serve in World War II. The Biggles stories were written as exciting adventures for boys about Biggles' war-time exploits and his work for the British Secret Service.

James Bond

The creation of World War II Intelligence Officer and novelist Ian Fleming (1908–1964), James Bond was a naval officer and spy, whose codename was 007. The Bond books have sold 100 million copies worldwide and were made into blockbuster movies in one of the most successful film franchises ever.

Sherlock Holmes

One of the most famous fictional Britons is Sherlock Holmes. He was created in 1887 by the author, Sir Arthur Conan Doyle (1859–1930). Holmes was a 'consulting detective' with an unrivalled ability to solve crimes and bring the guilty to justice. His skill lay in his great observational powers. He could tell a great deal about people, the work they did, where they had been and what they had been doing by noticing tiny clues that went unseen by most people.

Robin Hood

A legendary Medieval English hero, Robin Hood is said to have stolen from the rich and given to the poor. According to one story, he supported King Richard I, the Lionheart. While Richard was away fighting in the Third Crusade, his brother John ruled England. Robin did not support John and became an outlaw during his reign. A skilled archer

and swordsman, Robin and his band of merry men lived in Sherwood Forest, Nottinghamshire, although some early ballads locate him in Barnsleydale, Yorkshire.

Wallace and Gromit

Wallace and his dog, Gromit, are perhaps the most famous fictional Britons today. They are characters in animated films made by Nick Park (b.1958) of Aardman Animations. They are clay models filmed by a process called stop motion animation. One photograph is taken, the characters are moved a little, then another photograph is taken and so on.

Three films starring Wallace and Gromit – *The Wrong Trousers* (1993), *A Close Shave* (1995) and *The Curse of the Were-Rabbit* (2005) – won Academy Awards, or Oscars.

British villains

Not all Britons are remembered for good reasons. British history has its fair share of notorious villains. One of the most infamous is Guy Fawkes (1570–1606). Although he was actually prevented from carrying out his evil deed, he is remembered for what he planned to do. With others, he intended to kill King James I of England by blowing up the Houses of Parliament. He was discovered, tortured until he revealed the full story of the plot and then executed.

Dick Turpin

The notorious highwayman Dick Turpin (1705–1739) was a robber on horseback who preyed on travellers. While he was in prison under a false name for shooting his landlord's cockerel, he was identified and charged with horse theft. At that time, horse theft was punished by death. Turpin was found guilty and executed.

Jack the Ripper

One of the most infamous criminals was Jack the Ripper, who murdered at least five women in the Whitechapel area of London in 1888. No-one can say for certain that he was British, because he was never caught.

John George Haigh

Serial killer John George Haigh (1909–1949) murdered at least six people in the 1940s. He was nicknamed The Acid Bath Murderer, because he disposed of his victims' bodies by dissolving them in acid! When he was arrested, he admitted to his crimes under the mistaken belief that he could not be found guilty if no bodies were found. However, there was enough evidence to prove his guilt and he was executed.

The Kray Twins

Ronnie and Reggie Kray were gangsters who terrorised London's East End in the 1950s and 1960s. Their involvement in armed robberies, arson, violent assaults and murders led to their arrest in 1968 and imprisonment for life. Ronnie died in prison in 1995 and Reggie died eight weeks after his release in 2000.

The Great Train Robbery

In 1963, a group of criminals carried out a notorious robbery that became known as The Great Train Robbery. They stopped a mail train in Buckinghamshire and stole more than £2 million (worth tens of millions today). The train's driver, Jack Mills, was violently attacked and never fully recovered from his injuries. The robbers went on the run. One of them, Ronnie Biggs, escaped arrest until 2001, when he returned voluntarily from Brazil because of failing health.

Notorious political figures

John Profumo
The Conservative Minister for War, John Profumo (1915–2006), shared a mistress with a Russian spy, then lied about it to the House of Commons and had to resign. He spent the rest of his life volunteering for charity and was awarded a CBE in 1975.

John Stonehouse
Labour MP John Stonehouse (1925–1988) held several government positions before embarking on a series of unsuccessful business ventures. He then faked his own death in order to run away to a new life with his mistress.

Screaming Lord Sutch
David Edward Sutch (1940–1999) was one of the most colourful characters in British politics. He was a pop singer who founded a political party called The Monster Raving Loony Party. He contested more than 40 elections, rarely polling more than a few hundred votes, but adding fun to the proceedings. He was easily recognised by his outrageous clothes.

Pirates

Some of the most ruthless villains in British history were pirates. During the Golden Age of Piracy in the seventeenth and eighteenth centuries, British pirates attacked mainly Spanish ships bringing valuable cargoes home from Spain's empire in the Americas. Many of the pirates had served in the English navy. When the War of Spanish Succession ended in 1713, they found themselves out of work. Faced with poverty in England, they chose instead to seek adventure and wealth by becoming outlaws at sea. Some of them achieved fame, too. Blackbeard, Calico Jack and Captain Kidd are just three of the most notorious British pirates.

'Yo, ho, ho and a bottle of rum!'

'Dead Man's Chest', the well-known pirate song, is a fictional sea shanty originally from Robert Louis Stevenson's novel *Treasure Island* (1883).

Blackbeard

famous British pirates

Henry Morgan (c1635–1688)
Became the Lieutenant Governor of Jamaica.

Bartholomew Roberts (1682–1722)
The most successful pirate of the Golden Age.
Captured more than 470 ships.

Edward Teach ('Blackbeard') (c1680–1718)
A fierce pirate who went into battle with
smoking fuses sticking out from under his hat.

Anne Bonny (c1698–1782)
One of very few female pirates.

Henry Every (1653–c1699)
One of the few pirates who retired without
being arrested or killed in battle.

Jack Rackham ('Calico Jack') (1682–1720)
Named after his colourful clothes, made of
calico.

William ('Captain') Kidd (c1645–1701)
Rumoured to have left buried treasure, but it
has never been found.

William Dampier (1651–1715)
The first pirate to sail into the Pacific Ocean
and the first person to circumnavigate the
world three times.

CHAPTER ONE

SCIENTISTS AND ENGINEERS

British scientists discovered many of the laws of nature that underpin science today. British engineers developed the steam engine, railways and steamships. British physicians and medical researchers developed vaccination and new antibiotics. British cosmologists developed new theories about how the universe began. And Darwin produced his controversial theory of evolution.

Robert Hooke (1635–1703)

A brilliant seventeenth century scientist. Hooke devised Hooke's Law, which describes the way materials stretch. He studied optics and gravity, although this work was overshadowed by Sir Isaac Newton's. He also wrote the first blockbuster science book – *Micrographia* – about his discoveries with a microscope.

Hooke invented the universal joint, the balance wheel used in watches and the iris diaphragm used in camera lenses. He also thought of using the word 'cell' to describe the building blocks of plants and animals. He was an architect and he also made discoveries in astronomy. He had several bitter arguments with other scientists, especially Sir Isaac Newton, and his reputation suffered as a result.

Sir Isaac Newton (1643–1727)

One of the most brilliant scientists who ever lived. Newton devised laws of motion and gravitation and carried out ground-breaking work in mathematics and optics. He built the first practical reflecting telescope. He studied the speed of sound, discovered that 'white light' is composed of all the colours of the rainbow and developed a theory of what light itself is. He set out his ideas and discoveries in two of the most important science books ever written – the *Principia* and *Opticks*.

Newton explained his genius by saying, 'If I have seen farther, it is by standing on the shoulders of giants.' However, he wasn't so generous towards other scientists in his own time. He was very intolerant of any criticism of his work.

Thomas Newcomen (1664–1729)
Invented the first practical steam engine, which led to the Industrial Revolution. Until the steam engine was invented by Newcomen in 1712, machines were powered by the wind (using windmills) or water (using water wheels). Windmills worked only when the wind blew hard enough, and water wheels could only be used near a river. Steam engines could be built anywhere. Newcomen developed the steam engine to deal with flooding in tin mines in Devon and Cornwall. His engines pumped water out of the mines.

Edward Jenner (1749–1823)

Developed a vaccine for smallpox. Jenner trained as a doctor and surgeon. In his lifetime, smallpox was a deadly disease in Britain. About one in three people who caught smallpox died. As many as 80 percent of infected children died from it. Throughout Europe, it killed 400,000 people every year.

Jenner noticed that milkmaids rarely caught smallpox. He wondered if they acquired resistance by contact with cows suffering from a similar disease called cowpox. On May 14 1796, Jenner scratched pus from some cowpox blisters on a milkmaid's hand into the arms of an 8-year old boy, James Phipps. When he then deliberately injected the boy with smallpox (which would obviously not be allowed today) the boy did not catch the disease.

In 1959, the World Health Organisation embarked on a project to eradicate smallpox. In 1979, the world was declared free of smallpox – the first, and to date the only, human infectious disease that has been wiped out in nature.

Richard Trevithick (1771–1833)

Built the world's first working railway locomotive. Trevithick built steam engines that were a fraction of the size and weight of the giant engines common at the time, but just as powerful. These engines were able to propel themselves. Trevithick built a steam-powered road locomotive called *Puffing Devil* in 1801, and another road vehicle called the *London Steam Carriage*. Then he mounted a steam engine on wheels and turned it into a steam locomotive at the Pen-y-Darren ironworks in Wales. It made the world's first railway journey in 1804.

The Red Flag Act
A man waving a red flag had to walk in front of steam-powered road vehicles to warn people that they were coming.

In 1808, Trevithick built a locomotive called *Catch me who can* and gave the public rides on it for a shilling. The train ran on a circular track in Bloomsbury, London. The public weren't very excited by the idea of rail travel and so Trevithick decided not to build any more steam locomotives.

George Stephenson (1781–1848)

Built the world's first railway line to use steam locomotives. Trevithick's invention of the steam locomotive inspired other engineers and inventors to build their own locomotives. Stephenson built his first locomotive, *Blücher*, in 1814. It could haul 30.5 tonnes (33.6 short tons) of coal at 6.4 kph (4 mph). He went on to build more locomotives. The railway gauge (the distance between the rails) he used, 1.4 metres (4 ft 8.5 in), became the standard railway gauge throughout the world.

In the early 1820s, George Stephenson built the Stockton and Darlington Railway line to link Stockton with several collieries in northern England, and his son, Robert, built locomotives for it. When the world's first passenger railway line was being built between Liverpool and Manchester, a competition called the Rainhill Trials was held to find the best locomotive to haul the carriages. The Stephenson locomotive, *Rocket*, won.

Early steam engines often exploded because of poor boiler design.

Michael Faraday (1791–1867)

Famous for his inventions and discoveries in electricity and magnetism. Faraday, the son of a blacksmith, worked for a bookbinder in London. He was fascinated by the books that passed through his hands and read as many of them as he could. When he read an article on electricity in the *Encyclopedia Britannica*, he decided to become a scientist. Faraday would go on to build the first device to produce motion from electricity and magnetism – an electric motor. He also discovered electromagnetic induction – the production of electricity by using magnetism. This led to the invention of a variety of important electrical devices, including the electricity generator, transformer and solenoid. He also invented the Faraday Cage, a metal mesh box that stops electric fields from getting inside it.

Faraday was keen to share his enthusiasm for science with other people, so he gave public lectures at the Royal Institution in London. These lectures still continue today as the Royal Institution Christmas lectures for young people.

Many hands make light work, they say, but in Faraday's case, only two were required.

Isambard Kingdom Brunel (1806–1859)

The engineer famous for building the Great Western Railway, a series of steamships and several important bridges and tunnels. Brunel helped his father, Marc, to build the first tunnel under a navigable river – the Thames Tunnel in London. It opened in 1843. His father invented a device called a tunnelling shield that stopped the newly-dug tunnel from collapsing until it was lined with bricks.

Isambard also designed the Clifton Suspension Bridge across the River Avon. It had the longest span of any bridge in the world at that time. Construction began in 1831, but was not completed until 1864.

When he was made chief engineer of the new Great Western Railway, he wanted passengers to be able to buy a ticket in London and travel all the way to New York by his Great Western Railway and then his *Great Eastern* steamship. The London station where passengers would begin their journey, Paddington Station, was also designed by Brunel.

The passenger ships Brunel built were the biggest of their time. His first ship, the *Great Western*, was launched in 1837. It was a wooden paddle steamer. His next ship, the *Great Britain*, launched in 1843, was propeller-driven and had an iron hull. His biggest ship, the *Great Eastern*, was not successful as a passenger liner, but helped to lay the first transatlantic telegraph cable.

Other great bridge builders

Abraham Darby III (1750–1791)
Built the first ever iron bridge, at Coalbrookdale in Shropshire.

Thomas Telford (1757–1834)
Built the Menai suspension bridge in addition to numerous roads, canals and other bridges. The town of Telford in Shropshire was named after him.

Donald Bailey (1901–1985)
Invented the Bailey Bridge, a prefabricated bridge used by military forces to span gaps up to 60 metres (200 ft).

The above picture illustrates
Darwin's 'Ascent of Man'.

Charles Darwin (1809–1882)
The English naturalist who developed the
theory of evolution – that all species
descended from common ancestors by a
process of natural selection. Darwin spent five
years sailing the world on-board *HMS Beagle*,
studying geology and collecting samples of
creatures while the ship carried out its
mapping duties. When he returned to England
in 1836, he began to wonder if one species
could change into another and if this might
explain the variations between the creatures
he had seen. He collected more evidence to
support his theory over the next 20 years.

As he prepared to publish his theory, he received a scientific paper written by another naturalist, Alfred Russel Wallace (1823–1913), outlining his own theory of natural selection. Essays and letters written by both men were presented to the Linnean Society, which established that Darwin had been the first to think of natural selection. His book, called *On the Origin of Species*, was finally published in 1859. It sparked a heated dispute between followers of religion and science that has continued to the present day.

Darwin approached the prospect of marriage as methodically as his scientific work. He drew up a list of pros and cons. The factors in favour of staying single included – '*Not forced to visit relatives*' and, if he married, '*Anxiety and responsibility, less money for books*'. But he eventually married his cousin, Emma Wedgewood. Although genetics was not well understood at that time, Darwin wondered if marrying his cousin might have caused the ill health that several of his children suffered from.

Alexander Fleming (1881–1955)

The Scottish biologist who discovered penicillin, the first antibiotic capable of treating a variety of serious infections. Fleming, the son of a farmer, trained as a doctor and went into research at St Mary's Medical school in London. During World War I (1914–18), he served in the Army Medical Corps. After the war, he returned to research at St Mary's.

While he was studying influenza in 1928, he discovered the antibiotic (bacteria-killing) effect of penicillin by accident. He had left a dish of staphylococcus bacteria uncovered. Later, he noticed that some mould had grown on it. A ring around the mould had no bacteria growing in it – the mould was killing the bacteria. Fleming found that the mould was Penicillium, so he called the active substance it contained penicillin.

Biologists and doctors experimented with penicillin and some of them had success in treating infections. Mass production of penicillin began in time to produce millions of doses for troops in the last two years of World

War II. Until then, soldiers often lost limbs, not because of their wounds, but because of life-threatening wound infections that could only be dealt with by amputating the limbs. Penicillin enabled doctors to treat the infections and save the limbs. Fleming was knighted in 1944 and, with two other researchers, Howard Florey and Ernst Chain, he was awarded the 1945 Nobel Prize in Medicine. After the war, penicillin was made available to the civilian population.

Here Fleming discovers how to turn penicillium spores into one of the most important tools of modern medicine.

Taking the wee

Penicillin was so scarce in the early days that the urine of patients treated with it was collected so that the penicillin could be extracted and used again!

famous British aircraft designers

Geoffrey de Havilland (1882–1965)
The de Havilland aircraft company produced fighters in both world wars and the *Comet*, the first jet airliner.

Sir Frederick Handley Page (1885–1963)
The Handley Page aircraft company produced heavy bombers in both world wars, airliners between the wars, and the Victor jet bomber in the 1950s.

Sir Sidney Camm (1893–1966)
Chief Designer of the Hawker aircraft company, which produced aircraft ranging from the World War II Hurricane fighter to the postwar Hunter and Harrier jets.

R.J. Mitchell (1895–1937)
Designed the Spitfire, one of the greatest World War II fighters. Mitchell was Chief Designer for Supermarine. Among the aircraft he designed were seaplanes that won the Schneider Trophy air races and broke the world airspeed record. He is best remembered for the Spitfire. Over 20,000 Spitfires were built – more than any other British aircraft.

Frederick George Miles (1903–1976)
Designed several light aircraft and then a plane to make the first supersonic flight, although the project was cancelled before test-flights could begin.

Alan Turing (1912–1954)

A scientist, mathematician and computer scientist who helped to break secret enemy codes during World War II. Turing worked at the top secret Bletchley Park codebreaking centre during World War II. He developed a machine called 'the bombe' to break the coded messages created by German Enigma machines. He also thought about artificial intelligence and how to decide whether or not a machine was intelligent. He invented the Turing test. If a computer could make someone think he or she was communicating with a human being, then the computer could be thought of as being intelligent.

Turing's private life was unhappy. He was gay at a time when this was illegal in Britain. The authorities thought he was a security risk because he could be blackmailed, so he was not allowed to continue with his secret work. On June 8, 1954, he was found dead, having taken poison. In 2009, Prime Minister Gordon Brown apologised on behalf of the British government for the way Turing had been treated.

Francis Crick (1916–2004)

One of the discoverers of the structure of DNA, the complex molecule that stores the instructions for life. Crick and American biologist, James Watson (b1928), worked together at Cambridge University. Using the results of X-ray experiments with DNA carried out by Rosalind Franklin (1920–1958), Crick and Watson found that DNA was a large molecule with a spiral shape, called a double helix, with the two sides connected by links called base pairs. Their discovery, in 1953, began a revolution in biology. Crick, Watson and another researcher, Maurice Wilkins (1916–2004), were awarded the 1962 Nobel Prize in Physiology or Medicine for their work. Rosalind Franklin was controversially overlooked.

The first people to learn that the structure of DNA had been discovered were the customers of the Eagle pub in Cambridge. On February 28, 1953, Crick walked into the pub and announced that he and Watson "had found the secret of life".

Sir Patrick Moore (b.1923)

Astronomer, writer and broadcaster. Patrick Moore presented the first edition of the television programme, *The Sky at Night*, in 1957, six months before the Soviet Union launched the first artificial satellite, Sputnik 1. The programme has been broadcast once a month since then. Moore has presented every programme, apart from an edition in July 2004 when he was suffering from food poisoning, making him the world's longest serving television presenter.

An asteroid, 2602 Moore, was named in honour of Sir Patrick Moore in 1982.

He has written more than 70 books on astronomy and is a former president of the Royal Astronomical Association and Society for Popular Astronomy, which he also co-founded. He specialised in studying the Moon. The maps of the Moon that he drew were used by both the Soviet Union and the US space agency, NASA, to plan space missions including the Apollo manned Moon landings.

Stephen Hawking (b.1942)

Leading theoretical physicist and cosmologist. Stephen Hawking was born on January 8, 1942 – 300 years exactly after the death of Galileo Galilei, the Italian scientist described as the father of modern science. In his twenties, Hawking was diagnosed with an incurable disease called amyotrophic lateral sclerosis (ALS), a form of motor neurone disease. As a result, he was later confined to a wheelchair.

In 1979 he took up the post of Lucasian Professor of Mathematics at Cambridge University, a post that had been held by Sir Isaac Newton. He worked with the mathematician, Sir Roger Penrose (b.1931), on theories that describe black holes and the Big Bang. It was thought that nothing could possibly escape from a black hole, not even light. However, Hawking developed a theory that allowed radiation, called Hawking radiation, to escape from a black hole.

In 1985, Hawking underwent an operation that ended his ability to talk. A speech synthesiser was built for him, giving him a distinctive electronic voice.

In 1988, he wrote a popular science book about cosmology called *A Brief History of Time*, which became an unexpected best-seller, having sold more than 9 million copies.

Black holes, which are thought to be at the centre of most galaxies, are better understood today because of Hawking's work.

Dame Jocelyn Bell Burnell (b.1943)

An astrophysicist who discovered pulsars. In 1967, Belfast-born Bell was working on her PhD in radio astronomy at Cambridge University when she discovered a strange radio signal coming from outside the solar system. The regular, repeating signal did not look natural. To begin with, it was labelled 'LGM1' (Little Green Men 1). When more of these signals were discovered, it seemed unlikely that different civilisations far away in space would transmit the same signal.

In fact, Bell had discovered a type of star called a pulsar – a rapidly spinning star sending out beams of radio energy that sweep across the sky like the beams of light from a lighthouse. In 1974, the Nobel Prize for Astronomy was awarded for the discovery of pulsars. Controversially, Bell did not receive a share of the award.

British women in science

Elizabeth Garrett Anderson (1836–1917)
The first woman to gain a medical qualification in Britain. She also created a medical school for women.

Beatrix Potter (1866–1943)
The famous children's author was also a respected mycologist (a scientist who studies fungi).

Dorothy Hodgkin (1910–1994)
Used X-ray crystallography to discover the structure of penicillin, vitamin B12 and insulin.

Rosalind Franklin (1920–1958)
Probed DNA with X-rays, providing Francis Crick and James Watson with the information they needed to work out the structure of DNA.

Yvonne Barr (b.1932)
Virologist who, with Michael Epstein, discovered a new virus that was named after them – the Epstein-Barr virus.

Baroness Susan Greenfield (b.1950)
A scientist, writer, broadcaster and member of the House of Lords whose research specialised in the human brain.

CHAPTER TWO

INVENTORS

British inventors have thought up everything from the telephone, television and jet engine to the communications satellite, World Wide Web and wind-up radio. And Charles Babbage designed computers in the nineteenth century!

Babbage's first Difference Engine, if completed, would have had 25,000 parts, weighed 15 tonnes and stood 2.4 metres (almost 8 feet) high – not exactly a pocket calculator!

Charles Babbage (1791–1871)

Invented the programmable computer. Babbage designed mechanical computing machines called the Difference Engine, Difference Engine No.2 and an even more complicated machine called the Analytical Engine. The Analytical Engine was designed to be programmed by using punched cards. None of these machines were completed in Babbage's lifetime, probably because the parts could not be made with enough precision by Victorian industry. Ada Lovelace wrote what we would call a program for Babbage's Analytical Engine, so she is recognised as the world's first computer programmer.

The Science Museum in London built a Difference Engine No.2 between 1989 and 1991. It was built to commemorate the 200th year of Babbage's birth. When the first calculation was made with it, the answer was accurate to 31 digits – better than a modern pocket calculator!

John Harrison (1693–1776)

Solved the problem of calculating longitude at sea. A ship's position is given by two numbers – its latitude (how far north or south of the equator it is) and its longitude (how far east or west of Greenwich, London, it is). Longitude cannot be found without knowing the time very accurately. Harrison spent 45 years developing clocks that were accurate enough to calculate longitude at sea.

Alexander Graham Bell (1847–1922)

Teacher of the deaf and inventor credited with inventing the telephone. Bell had a lifelong interest in elocution and speech. In 1870, his family moved to Canada and, the next year, he moved to the USA and became the professor of vocal physiology at Boston University. Meanwhile, he experimented with ways to transmit speech.

> Bell was made a chief of the Mohawk Indian tribe for inventing a way to write down their speech (they had no written language).

In 1876, Bell made the first ever telephone call by his prototype telephone to his assistant, Thomas Watson, in the next room – *'Mr Watson, come here, I want you'*. Bell and another inventor, Elisha Gray, submitted their ideas for the telephone to the US Patent Office on the same day. Bell was awarded the patent and went down in history as the inventor of the telephone. Other inventors who may have invented the telephone before Bell include an Italian inventor, Antonio Meucci, and a German inventor, Johann Philipp Reiss.

John Logie Baird (1888–1946)

Invented the world's first working television system. In the early 1900s, inventors were working on ways to send and receive moving pictures over long distances. By 1924, Baird had the first working system. It was a mechanical system that produced a fuzzy 30-line picture, 5 pictures a second (compared to 1080 lines and 50 or 60 pictures a second for high-definition television today). The BBC transmitted experimental television programmes using the Baird system between 1929 and 1935. The Baird system was soon replaced by electronic television systems developed by the EMI company in Britain and Philo Farnsworth in the USA. Baird went on to demonstrate colour television in 1939 and even 3D television in 1941.

People could buy Baird 'Televisors' as a kit, which they put together themselves. The kit was cheaper than a fully built Televisor, which cost £26 – too much for most people to afford.

Sir Frank Whittle (1907–1996)

Invented the jet engine. While Frank Whittle was training as a Royal Air Force pilot in the 1920s, he was already thinking about jet-powered aircraft. When he sent his suggestion for a jet engine to the Air Ministry in 1929, it was thought to be impractical. He patented his invention in 1930, but the patent lapsed because he could not afford to pay a £5 fee to renew it. In 1936, he formed a company called Power Jets, which built a working engine in 1937. An experimental jet-powered Gloster aircraft made its first flight in 1941.

Meanwhile in Germany, Hans von Ohain had independently developed a jet engine. Germany achieved the first jet-powered flight in 1939, before Whittle. Germany also produced the first jet-fighter, the Messerschmitt Me-262, but it arrived too late and in too few numbers to change the outcome of World War II. In 1948, Whittle was knighted and awarded a payment of £100,000 in recognition of his work.

Sir Christopher Cockerell (1910–1999)

Developed the hovercraft. People had been trying to build craft that moved along on a cushion of air since the eighteenth century, but Cockerell was the first to solve the engineering problems. He built models to check that the craft would work and he invented the name hovercraft for them. His first full-size hovercraft was the Saunders-Roe Nautical 1 (SRN1), which was built in 1959. It crossed the English Channel later the same year.

Sir Arthur C Clarke (1917–2008)

Foresaw the geostationary communications satellite, which is used by satellite communications and satellite television today. In 1945, in an article in *Wireless World* magazine, Clarke suggested using satellites in geostationary orbit for communication. A satellite in a geostationary orbit, 36,000 km (22,370 miles) above the equator, appears to hang motionless in the same position in the

Heavyweight hovercraft

The world's biggest civil hovercraft was the Saunders-Roe Nautical 4 (SRN4). The biggest version, the Mark 3, weighed up to 320 tonnes and could carry 418 passengers and 60 cars at a speed of up to 120 kph (75 mph). It was powered by four Rolls-Royce marine turbine engines fitted with massive 6.4 m (21 ft) steerable propellers. SRN4s carried passengers across the English Channel between 1968 and 2000.

sky, because the satellite takes 24 hours to orbit Earth and so keeps pace with the spinning planet. This means that radio dishes on Earth don't have to track the satellite as it moves across the sky. The dish is fixed in one position. This orbit is also known as the Clarke orbit. Clarke never tried to patent his idea, because he said he never thought it would happen in his lifetime.

Sir Alec Jeffreys (b.1950)

Invented DNA profiling, which has brought thousands of criminals to justice all over the world, and also exonerated innocent people accused of crimes. Jeffreys' interest in science began when his father gave him a chemistry set and a Victorian brass microscope. He graduated from Oxford University in 1972 with a first class degree in biochemistry. While he was working at Leicester University in 1984, he discovered a way to compare DNA from different people. He immediately realised that this could be used to prove family relationships between people and also to compare DNA collected from a crime scene with DNA samples from suspects. The technique is called DNA profiling, but it is also known as genetic fingerprinting.

In 1988, DNA profiling was used for the first time anywhere in the world to identify a murderer, when Colin Pitchfork was proved to have murdered two girls in Leicestershire, England.

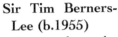

Sir Tim Berners-Lee (b.1955)

Invented the World Wide Web. Inventions today are usually the work of multiple people working together, but the World Wide Web was the invention of just one person – Tim Berners-Lee. The Internet had been in use in one form or another since the 1960s, but it was difficult to use. In the 1980s, while working at CERN, the European nuclear energy research organisation, Tim Berners-Lee thought of a way for scientists to share information more easily on the Internet. He thought of linking documents on the Internet to each other, so that it would be easy to jump from one document to another without having to know where the documents were physically stored – the World Wide Web. It was made available to the public in 1991. Today, there are more than 100 million websites containing more than 25 billion pages.

Other famous British inventors

Jethro Tull (1674–1741) Invented an improved seed drill, a machine for sewing seeds.

Abraham Darby (1678–1717) Invented a new type of blast furnace for producing iron.

Sir Richard Arkwright (1733–1792) Invented the spinning frame, which increased the production of textiles in factories.

Sir George Cayley (1773–1857) Built the first successful man-carrying glider.

Sir Humphry Davy (1778–1829) Invented the Davy Lamp, a safety lamp for use in mines.

William Fox Talbot (1800–1877) Invented the calotype photographic process.

Sir Henry Bessemer (1813–1898) Invented the Bessemer process for making steel.

Sir Joseph Swan (1828–1914) Invented the incandescent electric light bulb.

John Boyd Dunlop (1840–1921) Invented the first practical and successful pneumatic (air-filled) tyres.

Percy Shaw (1890–1976) Invented reflective road studs known as cat's eyes.

Trevor Baylis (b.1937) Invented the wind-up radio.

Sir James Dyson (b.1947) Invented the bagless vacuum cleaner using cyclone technology.

CHAPTER THREE

EXPLORERS AND ADVENTURERS

From the sixteenth century onwards, explorers and adventurers set out from the British Isles to discover new lands and islands. Many of these territories became part of the British Empire, which made Britain one of the first major world powers.

Sir Francis Drake (1540–1596)

Second in command of the English fleet that defeated the Spanish Armada and led the first circumnavigation of the world. Drake began his sea-going career as a merchant, trading in all sorts of cargoes, including slaves. However, his voyages often suffered attacks by Spanish ships, giving him a life-long hatred of the Spanish.

He led raids on Spanish ports in the Caribbean and seized Spanish cargoes. In 1577, Queen Elizabeth I sent him to attack Spanish ships and ports in the Pacific Ocean. He became the first Englishman to sail through the Magellan Strait at the southern tip of South America from the Atlantic to the Pacific. He returned to England in 1580 by continuing westwards, making him the first Englishman to circumnavigate the globe. He left England with five ships, but only one of them, the *Pelican*, completed the round-the-world voyage. Drake renamed the ship the *Golden Hind*. On his return, Queen Elizabeth I knighted him.

He continued to be a thorn in the side of the Spanish, sacking Spanish cities in the West Indies and on his way home, destroying up to 30 warships at Cadiz that the Spanish were preparing for war against England. When the Spanish did attack, in 1588, he served as the second in command of the English fleet that defeated the Spanish Armada. His final voyage to the West Indies, to attack the Spanish again, was a disaster. Drake died of dysentery during the voyage. He was buried at sea inside a lead casket.

Drake took a drum around the world with him. It is said that the drum was beaten to call the crew to action stations for battle. Today, it hangs in Buckland Abbey in Devon, Drake's former home. There is a legend that if the drum is heard beating, the spirit of Drake will return to help defend the country. There were reports that it was heard beating during both world wars.

Raleigh

Drake

Sir Walter Raleigh (c1552–1618)
Elizabethan adventurer and explorer. Raleigh
came to the notice of Queen Elizabeth I when
he helped to put down a rebellion in Ireland.
He became a firm favourite of the queen. In
the 1580s, he tried twice to establish a colony
in America and name it after the queen, but
both colonies failed. The queen recognised his
service and loyalty with a knighthood. He
played a part in the successful defence of
England against the Spanish Armada in 1588.
However, in 1591 he secretly married one of
the queen's ladies-in-waiting. When the queen
discovered the secret marriage, she had

Raleigh imprisoned in the Tower of London. When he was released, he sailed for South America to search for the fabled city of gold, El Dorado, but he failed to find it. When the queen died in 1603, the new king, James I, had Raleigh imprisoned and put on trial for treason. He was found guilty and sentenced to death, but this was reduced to life imprisonment. He spent 12 years in the Tower of London. While there, he wrote the first volume of *The Historie of the World* about ancient Greece and Rome. When he was released in 1616, he led a second expedition to look for El Dorado. During this voyage, his son was killed in an attack on a Spanish settlement on the Orinoco River. The attack outraged the Spanish ambassador to England, who persuaded the king to reinstate Raleigh's death sentence. Raleigh was beheaded on October 29, 1618. His head was presented to his wife, who kept it in a cupboard to show his admirers.

Raleigh is said to have brought potatoes and tobacco to Europe from the New World, although some accounts credit the Spanish with introducing them to Europe before Raleigh.

Captain James Cook (1728–1779)

Explored and mapped Newfoundland, the Pacific Ocean, Australia and New Zealand. Cook was born near Middlesbrough in Yorkshire. When he was a teenager, he moved to Whitby, a coastal town. He took a job on a collier, a coal ship, called the *Freelove*. He rose to the rank of ship's master. In 1755 he joined the Royal Navy. While serving on the *Eagle* in North American waters, he was trained in surveying and chart-making. He returned to England in 1762.

In 1769, Cook commanded the Royal Navy Research Vessel *HMS Endeavour* to observe the planet Venus crossing in front of the Sun – a rare event that was only visible from the southern hemisphere. Astronomers wanted it observed and recorded, because it would enable them to calculate the distance between the Earth and the Sun. After this, Cook carried on across the Pacific to New Zealand. He sailed around New Zealand and mapped most of it, before continuing on to Australia. *Endeavour*'s crew were the first Europeans ever to see Australia's east coast. He sailed along the coast and mapped it. He went ashore at a bay, which he named Botany Bay, and claimed the land for England. He returned home after three years.

His second great voyage (1772–1775) saw him visit Antarctica and Easter Island. His third voyage (1776–1779) searched for the Northwest Passage – a sea route between the Atlantic and Pacific Oceans to the north of North America. He searched from the Pacific side of the continent. Having failed, he sailed for the Sandwich Islands (Hawaii today). While he was trying to capture a local chief to persuade the natives to return a stolen boat, Cook was attacked and killed. The Cook Islands in the South Pacific Ocean were named after him.

Robert Falcon Scott (1868–1912)

'Scott of the Antarctic', a famous polar explorer. Scott joined *HMS Britannia*, an officer training college, in 1880 and then served on a series of Royal Navy vessels. In 1899, he was appointed by the Royal Geographical Society to lead an expedition to Antarctica. This expedition, known as the Discovery Expedition after the ship they used, left Britain in 1901. The men walked further south than anyone had ever gone before. They got to within 850 km (530 miles) of the South Pole and discovered a vast, flat expanse of ice called the Polar Plateau, or Antarctic Plateau. Scott's achievement made him a hero on his return to Britain in 1904.

By 1909, Scott was planning a second expedition to be the first to reach the South Pole. It became known as the Terra Nova Expedition, after its ship. The team left Britain in June 1910. They planned to use horses, dogs and men to haul sledges and they also took motorised sledges. When they began the trek south, the horses and motor-sledges proved to be failures and were left behind. The dogs were sent back after another month, leaving the men to haul the sledges the rest of the way. When the last support team was sent back, five men were left to carry on. They reached the South Pole on January 16, 1912, only to find that the Norwegian explorer Roald Amundsen had got there first. Scott was devastated.

On their return journey, their health worsened. One of the team, Edgar Evans, died. Another, Lawrence Oates, could hardly walk. He left their tent, saying, *'I am just going outside and may be some time.'* He walked outside into a blizzard, knowing that he would die, so that he would not slow the others down and risk their survival. However, the others died of starvation and exposure a few days later. Their frozen bodies were found in their tent.

The game of cards was more than a little *tents*.

Ernest Shackleton
(1874-1922)

Anglo-Irish explorer of the Antarctic. Shackleton had taken part in Scott's Discovery Expedition to the Antarctic, but had to leave it because of ill health. In 1907, he led his own expedition, the Nimrod Expedition, to Antarctica. He was trying to get to the South Pole, which no-one had managed yet, but he had to turn back only about 160 km (100 miles) from the pole. When he returned to England, he was rewarded with a knighthood.

Amundsen and Scott reached the South Pole before he could try again. For his next expedition, he aimed to cross Antarctica from north to south. While Shackleton and his team set out from the north, a second team would lay supplies on the other side of the continent. These would enable Shackleton's team to complete the crossing.

Shackleton's ship, *Endurance*, became trapped in sea ice. The pressure of the ice crushed the ship's hull and the expedition had to abandon it. The men lived on drifting ice for six months. When the floe they were on started breaking up, they took to their ship's lifeboats and managed to reach Elephant Island.

Shackleton and five others set out in one of the boats on a 1,300-km (800-mile) voyage to South Georgia, which was an extraordinary feat of seamanship in a small open boat. Shackleton and two others then made the first known crossing of South Georgia to reach a whaling station. A boat was sent from there to pick up the other three crewmen. Because of the sea ice, it was another three months before a ship could reach Elephant Island and rescue the crew.

Shackleton was on his way south to lead another Antarctic expedition when he suffered a heart attack in Rio de Janeiro. He refused medical treatment and carried on. Within hours of his arrival at South Georgia, he suffered another heart attack and died.

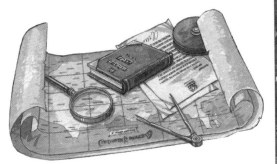

Shackleton's navigation kit, complete with map, dividers and magnifying glass.

British sailors who achieved firsts and set records

Sir Francis Chichester (1901–1972)
The first person to sail single-handed around the world by the old clipper ship route, and the fastest circumnavigation (1966–7).

Sir Alec Rose (1908–1991)
Sailed around the world on his own (1967–8).

Sir Robin Knox-Johnston (b.1939)
The first person to sail around the world single-handed and non-stop (1968–9). The oldest round-the-world sailor at the age of 68 (2007).

Sir Chay Blyth (b.1940)
Rowed across the Atlantic Ocean with John Ridgway (1966). The first person to sail non-stop around the world westwards (1971).

Dame Ellen MacArthur (b.1976)
Set records for the fastest single-handed monohull east-west transatlantic crossing by a woman, the fastest single-handed non-stop round-the-world monohull voyage by a woman, the fastest west-east transatlantic crossing by a woman and the fastest round-the-world solo non-stop voyage.

Mike Perham (b.1992)
The youngest round-the-world sailor in 2009 at the age of only 17.

Amy Johnson (1903–1941)

A pioneering pilot. While working as a secretary, Amy Johnson took up flying as a hobby. She gained a pilot's licence in 1929, and decided to make a record-breaking long distance flight. She would fly from Britain to Australia and try to break the record of 15 days. She persuaded her father and Lord Wakefield, the head of an oil company, to buy her a plane – a de Havilland Gipsy Moth, which she called *Jason*. She set off on her epic journey on May 5, 1930. It started well, but she was delayed by a crash landing and bad weather. She reached Australia on May 24. Although she didn't break the record, she was the first woman to fly solo from Britain to Australia and she was suddenly world famous.

More record-breaking flights followed during the 1930s, sometimes flying solo and sometimes flying with her new husband, another record-breaking pilot, Jim Mollison (1905–1959). When World War II began in 1939, she joined the Air Transport Auxiliary (ATA). She worked as a ferry pilot, delivering aircraft from factories to Royal Air Force bases.

On January 5, 1941, she was delivering an Airspeed Oxford aircraft to an RAF base in Oxfordshire when she crashed into the sea off the coast of Kent. She was spotted in the water, but a rescue attempt failed, and her body was never found. No-one knows exactly what happened. She was probably unable to land because of bad weather and flew east to find a hole in the clouds, but ran out of fuel.

Other British women fliers

Lady Mary Bailey (1890–1960)
The first woman to fly across the Irish Sea (1927).

Lady Sophie Heath (1897–1939)
The first woman to fly solo from South Africa to England (1928).

Sheila Scott (1922–1988)
Broke more than 100 aviation records, including the longest round-the-world flight – a 'world and a half' flight of 55,000 km (34,000 miles) in 1965.

Sir Ranulph Fiennes (b.1944)

Recognised by the *Guinness Book of World Records* as the greatest living adventurer. Fiennes has led more than 30 expeditions including exploring the White Nile by hovercraft (1969) and the Jostedalsbreen Glacier in Norway (1970). He made the first circumpolar navigation (circling the world from pole to pole) in the Transglobe Expedition (1979–1982) and found the lost city of Ubar in Oman (1992). He almost succeeded in making the first unaided crossing of Antarctica (1993), walking to the South Pole solo (1996) and walking to the North Pole (2000). Just four months after suffering a heart attack and undergoing a heart bypass operation in 2003, he ran seven marathons in seven days on seven continents. He climbed the Eiger in 2007 and became the oldest Briton to climb Mount Everest in 2009, despite having a fear of heights.

Sir Ranulph is related to the actors Joseph and Ralph Fiennes.

Other British explorers

Martin Frobisher (c1535–1594)
Made three voyages to search for the Northwest
Passage, a sea route between the Atlantic and
Pacific Oceans around Canada.

Sir John Franklin (1768–1847)
Disappeared in 1845 while searching for the
Northwest Passage.

Mungo Park (1771–1806)
The first Westerner to reach the Niger River.

David Livingstone (1813–1873)
A missionary and one of the greatest British
explorers of Africa.

Sir Richard Burton (1821–1890)
Known for his travels in Asia and Africa.

Henry Morton Stanley (1841–1904)
Journalist and explorer who found David
Livingstone, who was missing in Africa. He
also traced the course of the Congo River.

George Mallory (1886–1924)
Mountaineer, who disappeared while climbing
Mount Everest.

Andrew 'Sandy' Irvine (1902–1924)
Mountaineer, who disappeared on Mount
Everest with George Mallory.

CHAPTER FOUR

THEATRE AND CINEMA

Britain has a theatre tradition that stretches back to the days of William Shakespeare, more than 400 years ago. Today, British actors and directors work on stage, television and film all over the English-speaking world and they regularly win the industry's highest honours and awards.

Sir Charles 'Charlie' Chaplin (1889–1977)
One of the most famous and popular comic actors of the early years of cinema. Chaplin spent his childhood in desperate poverty in London. He spent a short time living in a workhouse (a home and work-place for people who could not support themselves) when his mother was too ill to work and his father had died.

The young Chaplin began his professional stage career at the age of 12 as a dancer with an act called The Eight Lancashire Lads. He toured the USA with Fred Karno's troupe of actors in 1910–1912. He returned to the USA soon afterwards and was spotted by Mack Sennett, a film director, who hired Chaplin. The little tramp character he played in dozens of silent movies quickly became a favourite with cinema audiences all over the world.

In 1917, he decided to make his own films. Two years later, he formed a new studio called United Artists with fellow actors Mary Pickford and Douglas Fairbanks and film director D. W. Griffith. He made several successful films with United Artists, including

Modern Times (1936), the last film to feature the little tramp.

He didn't make his first talkie (a film with sound) until 1940. It was a film called *The Great Dictator*, which ridiculed Adolf Hitler and the rise of Nazism in Germany. The film ended with Chaplin making an impassioned speech directly to the audience. It was a courageous film to make at that time.

When Chaplin visited England in 1952, his re-entry permit to the USA was withdrawn because of his political views. He made his home in Switzerland and didn't return to the USA until 1972, five years before his death.

Body snatched!

Charlie Chaplin's body was stolen from a Swiss cemetery in 1978 and held for ransom. The criminal gang was arrested and his body was recovered 11 weeks later. He was reburied under nearly 2 metres (6 ft) of concrete!

Stan Laurel (1890–1965)

An English comic actor who achieved worldwide fame with Oliver Hardy. Laurel started performing on stage professionally at the age of 16 under his real name of Arthur Stanley Jefferson. In 1910, he joined Fred Karno's troupe of actors and toured America with them. He was Charlie Chaplin's understudy. When he joined the Hal Roach studio, he changed his name to Stan Laurel. It was here that the Laurel and Hardy double act was born. They starred in almost 100 silent and talkie films over the next 20 years. When Oliver Hardy died in 1957, Laurel retired from acting. He died in 1965 after a heart attack. He had written his own epitaph – *'If anyone at my funeral has a long face, I'll never speak to him again'*.

Alfred Hitchcock (1899–1980)

A film director known as the master of suspense. Hitchcock's career began in silent films in the 1920s. *The 39 Steps* (1935) and *The Lady Vanishes* (1938) were so successful that Hitchcock was lured to the USA to make movies in Hollywood.

He created suspense in his films by showing the audience things that characters in danger couldn't see. His first Hollywood movie, *Rebecca* (1940), won the Oscar for best picture. His later films included three considered to be his best – *North by Northwest* (1959), *Psycho* (1960) and *The Birds* (1963).

Spot the director!

A trademark of Hitchcock's movies was his own brief appearances in many of them. He would appear, usually for just a few seconds, in the background of a shot.

Laurence Olivier (1907–1989)

Often described as the greatest actor of the twentieth century. Laurence Olivier appeared in scores of stage, movie and television roles ranging from Greek tragedy and Shakespeare to Hollywood heroes and modern drama. He was the first artistic director of the National Theatre, which he also co-founded. He was knighted in 1947 and became Baron Olivier of Brighton in 1970. In his later years, he made cameo and supporting appearances in films.

British actors who achieved stardom in Hollywood

Cary Grant (1904–1986)

Ray Milland (1907–1986)

Sir Rex Harrison (1908–1990)

Stewart Granger (1913–1993)

Richard Burton (1925–1984)

Audrey Hepburn (1929–1993)

Sir Sean Connery (b.1930)

Dame Elizabeth Taylor (b.1932)

Sir Michael Caine (b.1933)

Dame Julie Andrews (b.1935)

Sir Anthony Hopkins (b.1937)

Sir Ian McKellen (b.1939)

Sir Patrick Stewart (b.1940)

Brian Cox (b.1946)

Gary Oldman (b.1958)

Hugh Grant (b.1960)

Tim Roth (b.1961)

Catherine Zeta Jones (b.1969)

Ewan McGregor (b.1971)

CHAPTER fIVE

ARTISTS

British art encompasses the landscapes of John Constable, Lowry's matchstick men, Henry Moore's abstract sculptures and Tracey Emin's unmade bed. British artists work in every style of painting, sculpture and drawing, from the most traditional fine art to the most avant-garde abstract and installation art.

William Hogarth (1697–1764)

One of the leading artists of his generation. Hogarth started work as an apprentice silver engraver and then set up in business as a printer. In his spare time, he trained as an artist. He painted the portraits of wealthy people. He is known best for his later work that often poked fun at politics and everyday life. His most famous works include *A Harlot's Progress*, *A Rake's Progress* and *Gin Lane*.

J.M.W. Turner (1775–1851)

A leading romantic landscape artist of the first half of the nineteenth century. Turner had a great talent for drawing at an early age. He became a member of the prestigious Royal Academy in 1802 at the age of only 26. He was a prolific artist, although his work was not liked by everyone during his lifetime. When he died, he left nearly 30,000 sketches and paintings to the nation. His style often gave an impression of colour and light instead of showing every detail. One of his most famous paintings, *The Fighting Temeraire*, shows an old wooden-hulled warship that had fought in the Battle of Trafalgar being towed to the breaker's yard by a steamship.

John Constable (1776–1837)

An artist known for his paintings of the countryside around his home in Dedham Vale, Suffolk. As a youth, Constable worked in his father's corn business. In his spare time, he sketched the surrounding countryside. In 1799, he began studying art and by 1802, he was good enough to exhibit his paintings at the Royal Academy. He had decided to become a landscape artist, but his realistic treatment of landscape was unfashionable in Britain, so he painted portraits to increase his earnings. He was better known in France, where his paintings won awards. His most famous paintings include *Dedham Vale* and *The Hay Wain*. In 1824, he was awarded a gold medal at the Paris Salon, a prestigious art exhibition.

The artist's attempt to recreate *The Hay Wain* was marred by a perfectly clear sky.

L.S. Lowry (1887–1976)

Known for his paintings of Salford populated by matchstick people. While the young Lowry worked in an accountancy firm during the day, he took art lessons in the evening. He went on to study at the Manchester Municipal College of Art and Salford School of Art. During this time, he developed the style he is famous for. Known as naïve art, it has a childlike appearance. He found the scenes and subjects of his paintings while walking the streets of Manchester as a rent collector.

By the 1930s, Lowry was exhibiting his work at the Royal Academy in London. He was an official war artist during World War II and an official artist at the coronation of Queen Elizabeth II. His life's work totalled about 1,000 paintings and more than 8,000 drawings. The Lowry Art and Theatre Centre in Salford houses the world's largest collection of his work.

Henry Moore (1898–1986)
Artist and sculptor known for his abstract
bronzes. Moore began his working life as a
teacher. After World War I, he attended
Leeds School of Art and then the Royal
College of Art in London. He was an official
war artist during World War II.

In 1943, he was commissioned to make a
sculpture of the Madonna and Child for the
Church of St Matthew in Northampton. He
went on to create many more mother and child
sculptures, often as large rounded abstract
shapes. He won the main sculpture prize at
the 1948 Venice Biennale, a major art
exhibition, which confirmed his international
reputation.

Henry
Moore's
'Oval with
Points'
(1968–1970)

Important modern British artists

Francis Bacon (1909–1992)
Known for his bold, tortured paintings of people.

Lucien Freud (b.1922)
Grandson of the psychoanalyst, Sigmund Freud, known for his paintings of friends and family.

Peter Blake (b.1932)
One of the best-known British pop artists, designed the cover of The Beatles' album *Sgt Pepper's Lonely Hearts Club Band*.

David Hockney (b.1937)
Artist and stage designer.

Damien Hirst (b.1965)
Became famous for his series of artworks in which he preserved dead animals in formaldehyde.

Grayson Perry (b.1960)
English artist known as much for cross-dressing as for the vases and tapestries he makes.

Tracey Emin (b.1963)
A YBA (Young British Artist) whose work includes needlework, sculpture, drawing, installation art, photography, video and painting.

CHAPTER SIX

THE WORLD OF MUSIC

I n 1904, a German writer described Britain as 'a land without music'. In fact, Britain has a 1,000-year musical history stretching from early church music to great composers such as Elgar and Vaughan Williams, and on to world-famous pop and rock musicians like The Beatles and The Rolling Stones.

Sir Edward Elgar (1857–1934)

An English composer known for his orchestral works. Elgar studied music from a very young age. He was taking piano and violin lessons by the time he was eight. He began composing his own music when he was about 10 years old. He gave public performances on violin and piano, and gave music lessons to others. After writing a series of moderately successful works, his *Enigma Variations* were an immediate hit. Soon after this, he wrote *The Dream of Gerontius*, his greatest religious work. He is probably best remembered for the first of the five *Pomp and Circumstance Marches*. Words, written by Arthur C. Benson, were set to part of this music, now known as *Land of Hope and Glory*. As well as composing music, Elgar was an accomplished violinist and organist. He was the organist of St George's Roman Catholic Church in Worcester for 37 years.

Ralph Vaughan Williams (1872–1958)

One of the greatest English composers, whose music is noted for its power and essential Englishness. Vaughan Williams' first major success came in 1910 with the first performance of his composition, *Fantasia on a Theme by Thomas Tallis*. His choral symphony, *A Sea Symphony*, was performed for the first time in the same year. He had even more success with his *London Symphony*. His only copy of the score was lost when it was sent to the conductor Fritz Busch in Germany in 1914. Vaughan Williams had to reconstruct it from surviving parts.

During his time in World War I, the sound of gunfire impaired his hearing, which gradually deteriorated until he was deaf in old age. He wrote nine symphonies in all, including his *Sinfonia antartica*, which was based on the score he wrote in 1948 for the film *Scott of the Antarctic*. He also wrote instrumental and choral works, operas, music for ballets, arrangements of hymns and scores for radio, television and films.

Gustav Holst (1874–1934)

An English composer best known for his *Planets* suite. Holst started composing music when he was about 12 years old. He was a frail child who suffered from asthma, but he learned to play the piano, violin and trombone. He later played the trombone professionally and worked as a music teacher to make ends meet until he could earn enough from his compositions. The *Planets* suite brought him international fame and recognition, but he was a shy man who hated publicity. After a bout of ill health in 1923, he stopped teaching to concentrate on composing music. In all, he composed nearly 200 works, including operas, ballets, choral hymns and songs.

Holst's name was originally Gustavus Theodor von Holst. During World War I, he dropped 'von' from his name to make it sound less German.

Benjamin Britten (1913–1976)

One of the greatest composers of the twentieth century. Britten was a prolific composer and was only 17 and still at school when he wrote his first major work, *Sinfonietta Op. 1, A Hymn to the Virgin*. Britten was a pacifist and, in 1937, he composed a *Pacifist March*. In the same year, he met the tenor Peter Pears, with whom he collaborated on musical works. Pears also became Britten's partner.

Britten wrote a series of operas, notably *Peter Grimes, Billy Budd, The Turn of the Screw* and *Albert Herring*. His most famous works are probably his *War Requiem* and *The Young Person's Guide to the Orchestra*. He co-founded an annual music festival in the Suffolk town of Aldeburgh, which is still held today.

Other notable British composers

Thomas Tallis (c1505–1585)
Prolific composer of church music.

Henry Purcell (1659–1695)
Organist and one of the greatest English composers.

Thomas Arne (1710–1778)
Wrote *Rule, Britannia!* with words from a poem by James Thomson.

Sir Arthur Sullivan (1842–1900)
A leading Victorian composer known for his collaboration with the librettist W.S. Gilbert on a series of comic operas.

Eric Coates (1886–1957)
English composer known for simple and memorable melodies.

Sir Malcolm Arnold (1921–2006)
Composer known for his dances and many film scores.

Sir Peter Maxwell Davies (b.1934)
Composer and Master of the Queen's Music until 2014.

Andrew Lloyd Webber (b.1948)
Composer of musical theatre, who had his first musical composition published at the age of nine.

When the conductor asked his orchestra to compose themselves, he should have known they'd start improvising.

Dame Vera Lynn (b.1917)

'The Forces' Sweetheart' during World War II. Vera Lynn began singing on stage at the age of seven. By 1935, still a teenager, she was singing with dance bands, making records and broadcasting on radio. By 1940, she had her own radio programme, called *'Sincerely Yours'*, in which she sang for servicemen fighting abroad. She toured Egypt, India and Burma, giving concerts for troops. In 1942, she recorded her most famous song, *'We'll Meet Again'*. The lyrics, looking forward to meeting again in better days, caught the mood of the time. Her popularity continued throughout the 1950s and she had her own television show in the 1960s. In 2009, at the age of 92, she became the oldest living artist to reach number 1 in the British album chart with the release of a compilation of her best songs.

ENSA (Entertainments National Service Association) provided entertainment for the troops during World War II. Many of the leading British actors, comedians and singers served with ENSA. Vera Lynn was one of ENSA's most popular performers.

The Beatles

One of the world's most successful pop groups. The Beatles were four young men from Liverpool – John Lennon (1940–1980), Paul McCartney (b.1942), George Harrison (1943–2001) and Richard Starkey (b.1940). They started playing in clubs, famously the Cavern Club in Liverpool, but as their fame and popularity grew, they played to bigger and bigger audiences. The excited behaviour of their fans, which involved a lot of deafening screaming, was nicknamed 'Beatlemania'. When they weren't touring and performing all over the world, they starred in films, notably *A Hard Day's Night* (1964) and *Help!* (1965). They also provided the soundtrack for an animated film called *Yellow Submarine* (1968), which featured cartoon versions of the Beatles.

In 1966, they stopped touring and concentrated on studio work. Their music became more experimental. Tensions within the group boiled over while they were recording *The Beatles* album (known as the *White Album*) in 1968. The discontent led to the group splitting up in 1970.

British musicians who have sold the most records

The Beatles	1 billion
Queen	300 million
Elton John	250 million
Led Zeppelin	200 million
Pink Floyd	200 million
Rolling Stones	200 million
Genesis	150 million
David Bowie	136 million
Dire Straits	120 million
Status Quo	118 million

Top ten British musicians and groups with the most number one UK hits

The Beatles	17
Cliff Richard	14
Take That	11
Spice Girls	9
Oasis	8
Rolling Stones	8
McFly	7
George Michael	7
Sugababes	6
Robbie Williams	6

WRITERS

Britons have written about their own world and others since Anglo-Saxon times, about 1,400 years ago. A list of notable British writers on its own would fill a book, and Shakespeare towers above them all. It is impossible to include here more than a handful of the many writers who entertain, inspire and inform readers today.

All the world's a stage.

William Shakespeare (1564–1616)

The greatest writer in the English language. Shakespeare wrote about 38 plays and 154 sonnets. He wrote and acted for a group of actors called the Lord Chamberlain's Men. They performed their plays at the Globe Theatre in London. He wasn't revered as a great author in his own time, but his reputation has grown ever since then.

What did Shakespeare look like? The only portraits that are known definitely to show Shakespeare and that have survived to the present day were created after his death. A few other pictures painted at the time are said to show Shakespeare.

The Globe Theatre

The Globe Theatre, where Shakespeare worked, was closed in 1642 by the Puritans. It was demolished in about 1644 and its location was forgotten and lost. It was rediscovered in 1989. A new Globe Theatre, a reconstruction of the original building, was built 230 metres from this location and opened in 1997. It was the first building with a thatched roof allowed to be built in London since the Great Fire of London in 1666.

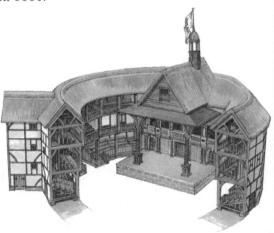

The motto of The Globe is '*totus mundus agit histrionem*' – 'all the world plays the actor'.

Samuel Johnson (1709–1784)

Author, essayist, critic, biographer and lexicographer. After looking for work as a teacher, Johnson moved to London and made his living from writing. In 1747, he was commissioned to write his greatest work, a *Dictionary of the English Language*. It was published in 1755 and was a great success, reprinted as it was several times during his life. Johnson was always short of money until he was granted a government pension. His reputation spread wider after the publication of the *Life of Johnson*, a biography written by James Boswell, a Scottish lawyer and friend of Johnson. Boswell toured Scotland with Johnson and both of them wrote about their travels.

Johnson was known for his wit and eccentricity. His many quotations include:

'Patriotism is the last refuge of a scoundrel.'
'Of all noises, I think music is the least disagreeable.'
'It is better to live rich than to die rich.'
'A cucumber should be well-sliced, dressed with pepper and vinegar, and then thrown out.'

Robert Burns (1759–1796)

Scottish poet and lyricist. Burns was born into a rural Scottish farming family. He started writing poetry when he was about 15. He had left school and was working as a farm labourer at this time. He wrote in the Scots language and also in the Scottish dialect of the English language.

The years 1784 and 1785 were fertile years for his poetry. He wrote some of his best-known poems at this time, including *Holy Willie's Prayer*, *To a Mouse*, *The Jolly Beggars* and *The Holy Fair*. He was planning to emigrate to Jamaica and to pay for the voyage by publishing a book of his poems. However, the book, known as the *Kilmarnock Edition*, was so successful that he changed his plans at the last moment and stayed in Scotland. The farmer-poet from rural Scotland was feted in Edinburgh society.

The 19th century scholar and educationalist J. S. Blackie said of Burns, '*When Scotland forgets Burns, then history will forget Scotland*'.

Burns worked with a music publisher to collect, preserve and publish traditional Scottish folk-songs. He wrote more than 100 songs himself, including *Auld Lang Syne*, which is often sung at New Year. He returned to farming and then trained as an Exciseman in Dumfries. In 1790 he wrote *Tam O'Shanter*, considered to be one of the best narrative poems (poems with a plot or that tell a story). Years of hard physical farm work eventually took its toll and he finally succumbed to a long-standing heart problem. He died at the age of only 37. In his short life, he had come to be regarded as Scotland's national poet.

'O, my luve is like a red, red rose, That's newly sprung in June.'

**Robert Burns
(1759–1796)**

Jane Austen (1775–1817)

Novelist known for her works of romantic fiction set among England's gentry. Austen started writing when she was only 11 years old. She wrote a selection of her stories, poems and plays in three notebooks, which are known as the Juvenilia. Her published novels, *Sense and Sensibility*, *Pride and Prejudice*, *Mansfield Park* and *Emma*, were well-received by the public. The Prince Regent, who ruled Britain and Ireland while his father, George III, was ill, liked Austen's books so much that he kept a set of them in each of his residences.

Austen fell ill in 1816, but continued to work. She died the following year. Two of her books were published after her death – *Persuasion* and *Northanger Abbey*. These books named Jane Austen as their author for the first time. Her other books were written by 'A Lady'. Austen's novels have been in print continuously since 1833.

Lord Byron (1788–1824)

English romantic poet. George Gordon, Lord Byron, is remembered as much for the excesses of a reckless life as for his literary work. He inherited his title when he was only 10 years old. During his teens, he ran up large debts and scandalised society with his love affairs. His first collection of poems, published in 1807, received poor reviews. Success came five years later with *Childe Harold's Pilgrimage*. After several more books, a tale in verse called *The Corsair* (1814), was a huge success, selling 10,000 copies on its first day. Rising debts and criticism of his private life drove him out of England for the last time in 1816. He lived in Geneva and then Italy until 1823, when he sailed to Greece. He planned to support the Greek campaign for independence from the Ottoman Empire, but he died of a fever before seeing action.

Lady Caroline Lamb, a novelist and Byron's former lover, said of him that he was *'mad, bad and dangerous to know'*.

Mary Wollstonecraft Shelley (1797–1851)
Novelist and creator of *Frankenstein*. While Mary Godwin (who later became Mary Shelley when she married the poet Percy Shelley) was on holiday with Shelley, Lord Byron and others near Lake Geneva, Byron suggested that they write stories of the supernatural. Mary's was *Frankenstein*. She intended it to be a short story, but Shelley encouraged her to expand it into the novel that became world-famous. When Percy Shelley died in 1822, Mary compiled a volume of his poetry, *The Complete Poetical Works of Percy Bysshe* (1824) and continued writing novels, poems and essays until shortly before her death.

Grrrrr!

Charles Dickens (1812–1870)

The most popular author of novels set in Victorian England, Dickens was born into a poor family in Portsmouth. He went to school at the age of nine, but when his father was sent to prison in 1824, Charles had to leave school and work in a factory. He worked ten hours a day for six shillings a week.

In 1827, he found work as a law clerk, but left soon afterwards to work as a court stenographer – someone who records everything said in a court of law. He went on to work as a shorthand reporter recording Parliamentary proceedings.

In 1833, he started writing sketches and essays, sometimes under the pen-name Boz. This led to his first novel, *The Pickwick Papers* (1836). It was very successful and more novels followed, including *Oliver Twist, Nicholas Nickleby, A Christmas Carol, David Copperfield, A Tale of Two Cities* and *Great Expectations*. He also wrote travel books and plays, and edited periodicals. He travelled widely and campaigned against slavery in the United States and poverty in Britain.

Child as he was, he was desperate with hunger, and reckless with misery. He rose from the table; and advancing to the master, basin and spoon in hand, said: somewhat alarmed at his own temerity:

Please, sir, I want some more.

Oliver Twist,
1838

The Brontë sisters

Three writers of romantic fiction. Charlotte (1816–1855), Emily (1818–1848) and Anne (1820–1849) Brontë grew up in Haworth, Yorkshire, which has become known as Brontë country. The sisters, who worked as schoolteachers and governesses, had written poems and stories since their childhood. They were already published poets when their first novels appeared in 1847.

Charlotte's *Jane Eyre* was the first, followed by Emily's *Wuthering Heights* and then Anne's *Agnes Grey*. They wrote under the pen-names of Currer, Ellis and Acton Bell. The books were successful, especially *Jane Eyre*. Unfortunately, Emily died the next year, in 1848. Anne published one more novel, *The Tenant of Wildfell Hall*, in 1848, and died the following year. Charlotte went on to publish two more novels, *Shirley* and *Vilette*, before her death. Her first (unpublished) novel, *The Professor*, was published after her death. Their novels have become classics of English literature and are still read and enjoyed today.

Sir Arthur Conan Doyle (1859–1930)
Scottish physician and writer who created the brilliant detective, Sherlock Holmes. Conan Doyle started writing while he was studying medicine in Edinburgh. His first story was published when he was 20. After he qualified as a doctor, he worked as a ship's doctor and then set up a practice in Portsmouth. In his spare time, he wrote stories. His first Sherlock Holmes story, *A Study in Scarlet*, was published in 1887. Holmes was based on Dr Joseph Bell, under whom Conan Doyle had studied medicine. Further Sherlock Holmes stories were published in *The Strand Magazine*. He also wrote a series of books about the exploits of Professor Challenger, a series of historical novels and more than 40 other books.

In 1917, two young girls produced photographs that were said to show fairies dancing. Conan Doyle, who was a spiritualist, believed they were genuine. The episode became known as the Cottingley fairies. However, in the 1980s, the girls admitted that the photographs were fake.

Rudyard Kipling (1865–1936)

Author and poet best-known for his *Jungle Book, Just So* stories and the poem *If–*. Kipling was born in British India. When he was five, he was taken to England, while his parents stayed in India. He attributed his enthusiasm for writing fables to the cruelty he experienced during this time. He was not thought to be clever enough to go on to university, so his father found him work as the assistant editor of a newspaper in Lahore (then in India, now in Pakistan). So, he returned to India at the age of 16. He described his 'English years' falling away, never to return.

In 1995, the BBC held a poll to find the nation's favourite poem. Kipling's '*If–*' won.

His first collection of poems was published in 1886. His editor asked him to write short stories for the newspaper and these were later published together in 1888 as *Plain Tales from the Hills*. The next year, he left India for London. He travelled the long way home, eastwards via the USA, writing stories on the way.

In 1892, he returned to the USA with his new wife and began writing what would become *The Jungle Book*. In 1896, the Kiplings left the USA again and settled in England. In 1901, *Kim* was published, followed the next year by his *Just So Stories for Little Children*. In 1907, he was the first English author to be awarded the Nobel Prize for Literature. He suffered from depression in his later years, possibly because of the loss of his only son, John, at the Battle of Loos during World War I.

India's Taj Mahal, one of the many aspects of the east which may have inspired Kipling's work.

H.G. Wells (1866–1946)

One of the most famous authors of science fiction novels. His early novels deal with topics common in science fiction today, but almost unknown in Wells' day – time travel (*The Time Machine*), human-animal experimentation (*The Island of Doctor Moreau*), invisibility (*The Invisible Man*), the arrival of aliens on Earth (*The War of the Worlds*), manned spaceflights to the Moon (*The First Men in the Moon*) and the future of warfare (*The Shape of Things to Come*). He also wrote a great deal of non-fiction.

In 1938, the American Mercury Theatre broadcast a radio play based on *War of the Worlds*, directed and narrated by Orson Welles. Presented as a series of simulated news bulletins, it was so realistic that large numbers of people believed that Martians really were landing on Earth.

A film of *The Time Machine*, released in 2002, was directed by Simon Wells, who was H.G. Wells' great-grandson.

Wilfred Owen (1893–1918)

The leading war poet of the First World War. Owen had been writing poetry since his youth, but his war service transformed his writing. His experiences during World War I were so traumatic that he suffered from shell shock, known as battle fatigue today. While recovering in Edinburgh, his doctor suggested that he write about his experiences. Then he met the war poet, Siegfried Sassoon, who influenced his writing. Owen could have

British First World War poets

Siegfried Sassoon (1886–1967) Known for his anti-war poetry.

Rupert Brooke (1887–1915) Known for his optimistic and idealistic war poems.

Robert Graves (1895–1985) Novelist and poet. Wrote realistic war poetry about life at the front line.

Edward Thomas (1878–1917) Writer who turned to poetry only in his last three years.

stayed in Britain, but he felt it was his duty to return to the front. While leading troops crossing the Sambre Canal near Ors, he was shot dead. The war ended just one week later. He is remembered for poems including *Dulce et Decorum Est* and *Anthem for Doomed Youth*.

Sir Salman Rushdie (b.1947)

A British-Indian author whose work explores the cultures and connections that link and divide people in the Eastern and Western worlds. Rushdie was born in Mumbai, educated in Britain and worked in advertising before becoming a full-time writer. His second novel, *Midnight's Children*, won the 1981 Booker Prize. It tells the story of a child born on the stroke of midnight as India gained its independence from Britain in 1947.

His fourth novel, *The Satanic Verses* (1988), caused protests in the Muslim world. Rushdie's life was threatened and he had to go into hiding.

Notable British poets

John Milton (1608–1674) Poet best known for his epic poem, *Paradise Lost*.

William Wordsworth (1770–1850) Co-founder of the Romantic Movement in poetry.

Samuel Taylor Coleridge (1772–1834) Co-founder of the Romantic Movement and one of the Lake poets.

Percy Bysshe Shelley (1792–1822) One of the finest lyric poets.

John Keats (1795–1821) One of the great romantic poets.

Alfred, Lord Tennyson (1809–1892) Poet Laureate from 1850 until his death. Wrote the famous poem, *The Charge of the Light Brigade*.

Sir John Betjeman (1906–1984) One of the most popular British poets. Poet Laureate from 1972 until his death.

W.H. Auden (1907–1973) Won the Pulitzer Prize for his poem *The Age of Anxiety*.

Philip Larkin (1922–1985) Offered the position of Poet Laureate in 1984, but declined.

Ted Hughes (1930–1998) Poet, dramatist, critic, and short story writer. Poet Laureate from 1984 until his death.

Benjamin Zephaniah (b.1958) Rastafarian novelist, playwright and performance poet.

Notable British authors

Geoffrey Chaucer (1343–1400) Best remembered for *The Canterbury Tales.*

Jonathan Swift (1667–1745) Anglo-Irish writer famous for *Gulliver's Travels.*

Thomas Hardy (1840–1928) Novelist and poet who wrote *Far from the Madding Crowd, Tess of the d'Urbervilles* and *Jude the Obscure.*

Robert Louis Stevenson (1850–1894) Wrote *Treasure Island, Kidnapped* and *The Strange Case of Dr Jekyll and Mr Hyde.*

J.M. Barrie (1860–1937) Creator of *Peter Pan.*

D.H. Lawrence (1885–1930) Author and poet who wrote *Lady Chatterley's Lover*, the subject of a famous obscenity trial in 1960.

Agatha Christie (1890–1976) Prolific writer of murder mysteries featuring the Belgian detective Hercule Poirot and amateur detective Miss Marple.

Graham Greene (1904–1991) Author of novels including *Brighton Rock, The Third Man* and *Our Man in Havana.*

Ian Fleming (1908–1964) Creator of James Bond.

J.K. Rowling (b.1965) Author of the Harry Potter books, which have sold more than 400 million copies and led to a series of successful films.

CHAPTER EIGHT

KINGS AND QUEENS

England's various tribes were unified under a single ruler, Offa, in AD 757. Since then, England, and then Britain, has had an almost unbroken line of kings and queens. Some of them were unremarkable. Others left an indelible mark on history.

Alfred the Great (849–899)

The only English king to be known as 'the Great'. Noted for his defence of England against the Vikings... and burning those cakes. Alfred became King when his brother, King Ethelred of Wessex, was killed at the battle of Merton. England was in the grip of a Viking invasion. After several defeats at the hands of the Vikings, Alfred was forced to make peace with them. However, the fighting started again. In one battle, Alfred was lucky to escape. According to legend, he was taken in by a peasant woman. She didn't know who he was and she left him to watch cakes cooking on her fire, but he let them burn.

At this time, Wessex was the only Anglo-Saxon kingdom that had not been conquered by the Vikings. Alfred fought back and repelled the Vikings, gaining more land in West Mercia and Kent. He went on to reorganise the army, navy, laws and taxation and he encouraged education. He also began the *Anglo-Saxon Chronicle*, writings that tell the history of Anglo-Saxon England. Copies were sent out to monasteries, which had to keep them up to date. Nine copies have survived to the present day. Alfred made English the official written language.

Grrr!

Henry V (c1387–1422)

English king famous for his victory at the Battle of Agincourt. Within two years of being crowned king of England in 1413, Henry faced a plot to unseat him. However, he was informed of the plot and its leaders were captured and executed. Henry turned his attention to France, where his forces captured Harfleur. Then, while his army was heading for Calais, a French army met them near the village of Agincourt. Henry's army defeated them in a famous victory. He followed this success by taking Normandy. In 1420, the French accepted Henry's claim to the French throne and he married Catherine of Valois, the French king's daughter. He died from dysentery during his next military campaign in France.

Henry was almost killed in battle in 1403 when he was struck in the face by an arrow. Its metal tip lodged deep in his face. His surgeon, John Bradmore, had a special tool made. It was pushed into the wound and screwed into the hollow arrow tip, then pulled out. In an era without anaesthetics, it would have been excruciatingly painful!

Henry VIII liked to
chop and change.

Henry VIII (1491–1547)
The English king known for his six wives and
creating the Church of England. Henry VIII
was England's second Tudor monarch. In his
youth, Henry was slim and athletic. He played
tennis and hunted on horseback, but as he
grew older, his health declined and he became
obese. He spoke French, Latin and Spanish,
played musical instruments, composed music
and wrote a best-selling book. The book, in
support of the Catholic Church, earned Henry
the title 'Defender of the Faith' from the Pope,
a title the British monarch still holds today.

It was essential for Henry to produce a male heir to succeed him as king. When each of his wives failed to give birth to a son, Henry found a way to end the marriage and move on to a new wife. Jane Seymour bore him a son, but she died two weeks later. When the Catholic Church refused to end Henry's first marriage so he could re-marry, he responded by breaking from the Catholic Church and establishing the Church of England, an event called the Reformation. He closed hundreds of monasteries across the country and took their lands and possessions, which were sold off.

The fate of King Henry VIII's six wives

Catherine of Aragon (1485–1536) Divorced

Anne Boleyn (c1501–1536) Executed

Jane Seymour (1508–1537) Died

Anne of Cleves (1515–1557) Divorced

Katherine Howard (c1521–1542) Executed

Catherine Parr (c1512–1548) Survived

Elizabeth I (1533–1603)

One of the greatest English monarchs, transformed England from an insignificant country to a world power. Elizabeth, daughter of Henry VIII, succeeded her half sister, Mary I, in 1558. She was a popular monarch. Her reign lasted 45 years and gave England a welcome period of stability. Theatres and drama flourished. Great voyages of discovery during her reign began an age of colonisation that eventually created the biggest empire in history.

> I would rather be a beggar and single than a queen and married.

Elizabeth is often depicted in paintings with a pale face and red hair – make-up and a wig to hide scarring and baldness caused by smallpox.

Spain and France both had ambitions to invade England. The most famous attack, by the Spanish Armada, occurred in 1588. The Armada was defeated. Elizabeth had rivals at home too. Mary Queen of Scots claimed the English and Scottish thrones. When she fled to England after an uprising against her in Scotland, Elizabeth had her imprisoned and, 19 years later, had her executed. Elizabeth never married.

Victoria (1819–1901)

Britain's longest reigning monarch. Victoria came to the throne in 1837 at the age of 18 when her uncle, King William IV, died. In 1840, she married her cousin, Prince Albert of Saxe-Coburg-Gotha. Over the next 20 years, their happy marriage produced nine children, many of whom married into the royal families of Europe.

Prince Albert's sudden death in 1861 devastated Victoria, who withdrew from public life. Her reluctance to appear in public for years made her unpopular and, remaining in mourning, she wore black for the rest of her life. She was persuaded to return to public view in the 1880s and her popularity grew again. In 1877, she became Empress of India when the government of India was transferred from the East India Company to the British Crown. Her Golden and Diamond Jubilees in 1887 and 1897 were marked by great public celebrations. Her death at Osborne House on the Isle of Wight was widely mourned.

During Victoria's reign, power began to move from the monarch to Parliament and the people. Modern party politics developed at this time too. The monarch became more of a neutral figure, above party politics. More people were allowed to vote during her reign. Victoria, or her photograph, was seen by more of her citizens than any previous monarch, because of the invention of photography and the growth in popularity of newspapers. She was also the first monarch to travel by train.

Brides in most parts of the world traditionally wear white on their wedding day. This custom was started by Victoria, when she wore a white wedding dress for her marriage to Prince Albert. Astonishingly, she was less than 5 feet in height.

CHAPTER NINE

GOVERNMENT AND MILITARY

Leading politicians and military commanders have the power to change the course of a nation's history, especially in wartime. Their statues in our towns and cities stand as monuments to their achievements. They are inscribed with names like Wellington, Nelson and Churchill.

Boudicca (?–cAD60)

British queen who almost defeated the military might of the Roman Empire. Boudicca was the queen of a tribe called the Iceni of East Anglia. She was married to the Iceni's king – Prasutagus. When the Romans invaded England in AD 43, they were content to let Prasutagus continue to rule.

When he died, he left a will stating his wish that his daughters should rule after him. The Romans ignored his will and ruled the Iceni themselves. The Iceni, led by Boudicca, and other tribes rebelled. They destroyed the Roman capital of Britain, Camelodonum (Colchester today). They also defeated the Roman Ninth Legion, which was sent to defend the town. They went on to destroy Londinium (London) and Verulamium (St Albans).

The historian Dio Cassius wrote, *'all this ruin was brought upon the Romans by a woman, a fact which in itself caused them the greatest shame'*. The crisis was so serious that the Roman Emperor, Nero, almost withdrew Roman forces from Britain. However, the Roman governor of southern England, Gaius Suetonius Paulinus, eventually defeated Boudicca at the Battle of Watling Street in AD 60 or 61. Some 80,000 tribesmen were killed with the loss of only 400 Romans. Boudicca is said to have poisoned herself rather than risk being captured.

Sir William Wallace (c1272–1305)

A hero in Scotland for leading a rebellion against the English. In 1296, the English king, Edward I, sent an army north to invade Scotland. At first, the English forces were successful. Then in 1297, William Wallace led an attack on Lanark and killed the English Sheriff. More fighting men flocked to join Wallace. They defeated the English at the battle of Stirling Bridge and then carried out raids in northern England. An English army confronted Wallace's forces at Falkirk in 1298. This time, the Scots lost and Wallace escaped to France. While he was away, the new Scottish king, Robert Bruce, made peace with Edward. A ransom was offered for Wallace, dead or alive. He was betrayed and captured near Glasgow in 1305, taken to London and put on trial for treason. He was found guilty and executed.

Sir Thomas More (1478–1535)

Lord chancellor of England, executed for refusing to deny the authority of the Pope. When the English king, Henry VIII, broke with the Catholic Church and established the Church of England, leading figures in the church and state were forced to choose whether to side with the Pope or the king in religious matters. More, who had been a devoted servant of the king until then, felt unable to denounce the Pope. He resigned as chancellor and continued to argue against the break with Rome.

More was arrested in 1534 and put on trial for treason. He was found guilty and sentenced to death by being hung, drawn and quartered. However, the king overruled the court and changed the sentence to death by decapitation. His body was buried in an unmarked grave at the Tower of London. His head was displayed on a pike at London Bridge. His daughter took the head before it could be thrown away into the River Thames.

Oliver Cromwell (1599–1658)

English soldier who played a leading role in making England a republic. When armed conflict broke out between King Charles I and Parliament in 1642, Oliver Cromwell, a member of Parliament, created and led a very effective cavalry force called the Ironsides. When the New Model Army was formed in 1645, Cromwell was appointed its second-in-command under Sir Thomas Fairfax.

Parliament finally defeated the Royalist forces in 1648 and the king was put on trial for high treason the following year. He was found guilty and executed. Cromwell was one of the 59 people who signed the death warrant. A republic called the Commonwealth of England was declared after the king's death and

Parliamentarians and Royalists do battle at Marston Moor, Yorkshire.

Cromwell was sent to Ireland to deal with English Royalists who had joined forces with Irish Catholics. His brutal crushing of resistance made him hated and feared. Land owned by Catholics was seized and given to English and Scottish settlers.

Back in England, Cromwell was so frustrated with the lack of political progress that he dissolved Parliament by force and made himself Lord Protector of England in 1653. He wanted to heal the wounds of the Civil War and give the country a period of stable government, which he achieved.

Cromwell died in 1658. The Monarchy was restored in 1660 with the coronation of Charles II. In 1661, Cromwell's body was dug up and 'executed', and his severed head was displayed on a pole outside Westminster Hall.

When Cromwell saw a flattering portrait of himself that the artist Peter Lely had painted, he is said to have asked Lely to paint another portrait with *all these roughnesses, pimples, warts and everything as you see me*. It gave rise to the phrase 'warts and all'.

John Churchill, 1st Duke of Marlborough (1650–1722)

English soldier and statesman. John Churchill joined the army in 1667, at the age of 17. While serving on-board the Duke of York's flagship, he was quickly promoted to Captain in the Admiralty Regiment. His success in a series of diplomatic and military enterprises resulted in him being made Lord Churchill of Eyemouth and colonel of the King's Own Royal Regiment of Dragoons. In 1685, he successfully put down the Duke of Monmouth's rebellion against the catholic king, James II.

When the Protestant William of Orange became king, Churchill switched sides and supported him. He was rewarded by being made Earl of Marlborough. He was one of the most effective military commanders during the Nine Years' War between France and the allied armies of Europe. However, in 1692, he was discovered to be in contact with the exiled King James and was stripped of his ranks and positions.

Six years later, he was recalled to military service and commanded allied troops on the Continent during the War of the Spanish Succession. In 1702, England declared war on France and Churchill was given command of English, Dutch and German forces. Early success resulted in him being made Duke of Marlborough. His victories at the battles of Blenheim, Ramillies, Oudenarde and Malplaquet marked him out as an extraordinary military commander. His health began failing in 1716, but he was able to oversee the construction of his magnificent family home, Blenheim Palace.

Winston Churchill, the British Prime Minister during World War II, was a descendant of John Churchill. He was born at Blenheim Palace – by mistake! His parents were staying at the palace when he was born several weeks earlier than expected.

Ring! *Ring!*

Horatio Nelson (1758–1805)

Naval officer famed for his victory at the Battle of Trafalgar. Nelson joined the Royal Navy at the age of 12 and rose through the ranks quickly. He was captain of his own ship by the time he was 20. At the outbreak of the French Revolutionary Wars in 1792 he was given command of *HMS Agamemnon* and then *HMS Captain*. It was during this time that he lost the sight of his right eye and his right arm in sea battles. After recovering in England, he returned to sea and defeated Napoleon's fleet at the Battle of the Nile in 1798. He was successful again at the Battle of Copenhagen.

In 1798, after the Battle of the Nile, Nelson met a young woman called Emma Hamilton in Naples and the two carried on an affair until Nelson's death even though both were married.

In 1805, the Franco-Spanish fleet left the port of Cadiz to meet the English fleet under Nelson, who was then a vice-admiral. The engagement took place at Cape Trafalgar. As the fleet prepared for action, Nelson sent a famous signal from *HMS Victory* saying, *'England expects that every man will do his duty'*.

The Battle of Trafalgar was Nelson's greatest victory, and also his last. A sniper on-board the French warship *Redoubtable* shot him. Just before he died, he said, '*Kiss me, Hardy*'. Thomas Hardy, *Victory*'s commander, knelt beside him and kissed him on the cheek. Nelson's body was preserved in a barrel of brandy and brought back to England. He was given a state funeral and laid to rest in St Paul's Cathedral.

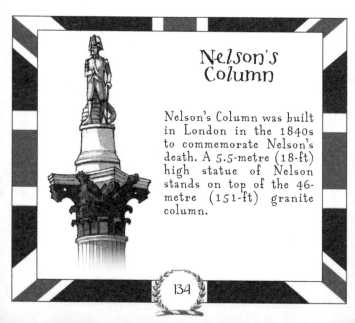

Nelson's Column

Nelson's Column was built in London in the 1840s to commemorate Nelson's death. A 5.5-metre (18-ft) high statue of Nelson stands on top of the 46-metre (151-ft) granite column.

Duke of Wellington (1769–1852)

One of the leading military and political figures of the nineteenth century. Arthur Wellesley was born in Dublin. He joined the army in 1787 and began his military service in Ireland. He was sent to fight the French in Flanders and then in 1796 he was dispatched to India, where his brother Richard was Governor-General. On his return to England in 1805, he received a knighthood for his victory at the Battle of Assaye in India and was elected to Parliament. He returned to Ireland as Chief Secretary for Ireland, but a few months later he left for Denmark, where he commanded an infantry brigade at the Second Battle of Copenhagen. In 1808, he was sent to Portugal to fight in the Peninsular War.

Wellesley returned as a hero and was created Duke of Wellington. He was also appointed British Ambassador to France. In 1815, Napoleon escaped from exile on the island of Elba and returned to France. Wellington took command of the British-Germany army and their allies. Wellington's army met Napoleon's near the small Belgian town of Waterloo.

Wellington, with Prussian forces under General Blücher, defeated Napoleon at the Battle of Waterloo, his most famous victory.

On his return to Britain, Wellington was given the position of Master-General of the Ordnance in Lord Liverpool's government. In 1827, he was appointed commander-in-chief of the British Army. The next year he became Prime Minister. His government lost power in 1830. When it returned to power in 1834, Wellington chose to serve as Foreign Minister under Prime Minister Robert Peel. He retired in 1846 and died six years later.

Wellington was an unpopular Prime Minister. He had to cover his windows with iron shutters to stop people from smashing them. It earned him the nickname, *'the Iron Duke'*.

Sir Winston Churchill
(1874-1965)

Soldier, politician, writer and British Prime Minister during World War II. Churchill attended the Royal Military College, Sandhurst, and then served as a soldier in India, the Sudan and South Africa. He also wrote newspaper reports and books about the campaigns. On his return to Britain, he was elected to Parliament as a Conservative MP in 1900. He fell out with the Conservative Party and switched to the Liberal party in 1904. By 1910 he had risen to the office of Home Secretary and then became First Lord of the Admiralty.

He had to resign in 1915 after being blamed for the disastrous Dardanelles campaign, when a massive attack on Turkish forces failed. He rejoined the army and served on the Western Front. He returned to government in 1917 as Minister of Munitions. In 1925, he switched back to the Conservative Party, now in government again, and was appointed Chancellor of the Exchequer.

During the 1930s, a period known as his 'wilderness years', Churchill was out of favour and out of office. His warnings about Germany's rearmament and the rise of Nazism went unheeded. When World War II broke out in 1939, Churchill was appointed First Lord of the Admiralty. When the Prime Minister,

137

Neville Chamberlain, resigned, Churchill replaced him at the head of an all-party government. His wartime speeches were a great inspiration to the British public and forces.

On June 18, 1940, after the fall of France, expecting the invasion of Britain to be next, he stirred the British people with a speech, which ended with, 'If the British Empire and its Commonwealth last for a thousand years, men will still say, 'This was their finest hour''.

On December 30, 1941, in response to the view of French Generals that 'In three weeks England will have her neck wrung like a chicken' by Nazi Germany, he said, 'Some chicken; some neck!'

Churchill was defeated in the first election after the war, but became Prime Minister again in 1951. In 1953, he was awarded the Nobel Prize for Literature. In 1955, at the age of 80, he resigned as Prime Minister because of ill health, but served as an MP until 1964. The following year he suffered a stroke and died. He was given a state funeral, which was attended by one of the largest gatherings of world leaders ever assembled. As his coffin made its final journey along the River Thames in London, crane jibs lowered in salute.

Coo!
Coo!

On June 4, 1940, Winston Churchill delivered one of the most defining speeches of World War II to the House of Commons of the UK Parliament:

'We shall go on to the end. We shall fight in France, we shall fight on the seas and oceans, we shall fight with growing confidence and growing strength in the air, we shall defend our island, whatever the cost may be. We shall fight on the beaches, we shall fight on the landing grounds, we shall fight in the fields and in the streets, we shall fight in the hills; we shall never surrender.'

Field Marshal Bernard Montgomery (1887–1976)

Famous British military commander during World War II. Montgomery went straight from school to the Royal Military Academy, Sandhurst, and then served with the Royal Warwickshire Regiment. During World War I, he served on the Western Front. After the war, he served in India, Egypt and Palestine.

At the outbreak of World War II, he commanded the British Third Infantry Division and then the Second Corps. In 1942,

Monty's double

A soldier and actor called Meyrick Edward Clifton James was employed as Montgomery's double. He appeared in various places as Montgomery and talked about fictitious military plans in the hope that he would be overheard by German spies. Clifton James wrote a book about his experiences and starred as both himself and Montgomery in a 1958 film of the book.

he was sent to take command of the Eighth Army in North Africa. Unlike other commanders, he often left his headquarters and got amongst his men, so that they got to know him.

He commanded the allied forces at the Battle of El Alamein against German and Italian forces, under one of the most experienced German commanders, Field Marshal Erwin Rommel. The battle lasted for 12 days and Montgomery won decisively. It was the first major land victory for the allies and was seen as the turning point of the war. Montgomery received a knighthood and was promoted to full general. At the end of 1943, 'Monty', as he was known, returned to Britain to help plan Operation Overlord, the allied invasion of Normandy. The invasion was successful and allied troops began their advance towards Germany. On May 4, 1945, Montgomery received the German military surrender. After the war, Montgomery was created Viscount Montgomery of Alamein. He continued in military service, becoming Deputy Supreme Commander of NATO forces in Europe from 1951 until 1958.

T.E. Lawrence (1888–1935)

Famous as Lawrence of Arabia. After Lawrence left Oxford University, he worked as an archaeologist in Syria. While he was there, he learned Arabic. When World War I broke out, he worked as an intelligence officer in Cairo. The British encouraged the Arabs to revolt against Turkey, which was allied with Germany. Lawrence, in Arab dress, fought with Arab forces under the command of Prince Faisal. His attacks on Turkish communication and supply routes tied up large numbers of Turkish troops. In 1917, his Arab forces captured the port of Aqaba. After the war, Lawrence travelled to the Paris Peace Conference to argue for Arab self-government, but he was over-ruled by a secret agreement between the British and French governments. Britain and France carved up the Middle East between themselves. Lawrence had become famous by then, but he was uncomfortable with celebrity. He tried to stay out of the public eye by joining the RAF under a false name, John Hume Ross. Then he joined the Tank Corps as T.E. Shaw before returning to the RAF in 1925. Just a few weeks after leaving the RAF in 1935, he died in a motorcycle accident.

The Man Who Never Was
In 1943, Allied forces were planning to invade Italy from North Africa. The invasion was to begin in Sicily. It was vital to make the German forces believe the landings would be made somewhere else, so that Sicily would not be heavily defended.

The body of a man, probably a 34 year old Welshman called Glyndwr Michael, was transformed into a man who had never lived – Captain (acting Major) William Martin of the Royal Marines. He was dressed in the right uniform and his pockets were filled with things the real Major Martin might be carrying – tickets, receipts, letters from home and keys. A briefcase chained to his wrist contained secret documents, which mentioned fictitious plans for Allied landings in Greece and Sardinia.

Major Martin's body was put into the sea from a British submarine, *HMS Seraph*, near the coast of Spain as if it had drifted away from a crashed plane. The body was found by fishermen and reported to a German agent in the nearby town of Huelva. When Spain returned the papers Martin was carrying, they were examined by the British, who discovered that the envelopes they were sealed inside had been opened and resealed. The Germans had read and believed the information in Martin's papers. As a result, German forces were concentrated in Greece, Sardinia and Corsica, not Sicily.

Noor Inayat Khan (1914–1944)
British spy in occupied France during World War II. The name Noor Inayat Khan is not as well-known as kings, queens, military leaders or prime ministers, yet she is one of the greatest Britons of recent history.

She was born in Moscow to Indian parents. She moved with her family to London and, later, to Paris. When France fell to Nazi Germany during World War II, she escaped to England. She joined the Women's Auxiliary Air Force (WAAF) and was then recruited by the Special Operations Executive (SOE). SOE trained her as a spy and radio operator. She was sent to occupied France to be the radio operator for a British spy network codenamed Prosper.

Many of Prosper's spies were captured and, with German forces closing in on Khan, she was given the opportunity to return to Britain, but she chose to stay in France. She moved around, transmitting messages to Britain and evading the German forces that were on her trail. Eventually, she was betrayed and taken prisoner by the Gestapo, Nazi Germany's secret police. She escaped from prison, but was recaptured. Despite being tortured repeatedly, she could not be broken and did not reveal anything she knew. She was sent to Dachau concentration camp, where she was executed. She was only 30 years old. Noor Inayat Khan was awarded the George Cross after the war in recognition of her amazing courage and service to Britain. She gave her life so that others might live in freedom.

The Baker Street Irregulars

The Special Operations Executive was a secret army of spies and saboteurs based in Baker Street, London. It was known as Churchill's secret army, the ministry of ungentlemanly warfare and the Baker Street Irregulars.

Margaret Thatcher (b.1925)
The first woman to be Prime Minister of the United Kingdom and the dominant political figure of the 1980s. Margaret Thatcher became active in politics while she was studying science at university. She was President of the Oxford University Conservative Association. She qualified as a barrister in 1953 and was elected to Parliament to represent Finchley in 1958. Within three years, she was given a junior government job at the Ministry of Pensions and National Insurance.

In 1970, she became Secretary of State for Education and Science. When the Conservatives lost power in 1974, she challenged Edward Heath for the party leadership and defeated him. In 1976, her scathing attacks on the Soviet Union earned her the nickname 'the Iron Lady'. She became Britain's first woman Prime Minister in 1979. The measures she introduced to tackle inflation and reduce government spending were very unpopular, but by 1982 the economy began to recover.

In the same year, Argentinean forces invaded the Falkland Islands. Peace talks failed and Thatcher sent a naval task force to recapture the islands, which was accomplished in two months. In 1984, as the government gathered in the Grand Hotel, Brighton, for the party's annual conference, an IRA bomb exploded in the hotel. Five people died and many were injured, but Thatcher delivered her speech the next day as planned. In 1990, Michael Heseltine challenged her for the party leadership. She survived the first round of voting but withdrew from the second ballot and resigned. She took a seat in the House of Lords in 1992. She had won three general elections in a row and was one of the first world leaders to raise environmental concerns including global warming, ozone depletion and acid rain.

> *'You turn if you want to. The lady's not for turning!'* The Iron Lady

Other notable British Prime Ministers

Robert Walpole (1676–1745) Britain's first Prime Minister.

Pitt the Younger (1759–1806) Britain's youngest Prime Minister at the age of only 24.

Sir Robert Peel (1788–1850) Helped to create the first modern police force.

Benjamin Disraeli (1804–1881) Prime Minister twice under Queen Victoria.

William Gladstone (1809–1898) Liberal Prime Minister four times – more than anyone else.

Neville Chamberlain (1869–1940) Tried in vain to make an agreement with Adolf Hitler to prevent war.

Clement Attlee (1883–1967) Created the National Health Service.

Harold Wilson (1916–1995) Dominant Labour politician of the second half of the twentieth century.

Edward Heath (1916–2005) Negotiated Britain's entry to the European Economic Community.

Tony Blair (b.1953) Won three general elections in a row, the longest serving Labour Prime Minister, but controversial because of the Iraq war.

CHAPTER TEN

SPORT

Some of the world's most popular sports, including football, cricket and lawn tennis, were invented in Britain. Unfortunately, foreigners have learnt to play these sports rather well too! Nevertheless, British men and women have achieved great sporting victories in these and many other sports.

W.G. Grace (1848–1915)

One of the most famous sportsmen of the nineteenth century. Grace was a doctor and was instantly recognisable because of his long black beard and towering stature – he was 1.87 metres (6 ft 2 in) tall. He is known as a cricketer, but he also played golf, lawn bowls and football, and was a 440-yard hurdler. Grace dominated the game, playing cricket for the MCC, Gloucestershire, London County and England. He played his last match in 1908 when he was 59. During his 43-year career, he scored 54,896 runs, made 126 centuries and took 2,876 wickets.

Sir Stanley Matthews (1915–2000)

A great English football player. Stanley Matthews was the first professional footballer to be knighted. His professional playing career spanned 33 years. He signed with Stoke City in 1932 and played his first international for England in 1934. In 1947, he transferred to Blackpool, but returned to

Stoke in 1961. He retired as a player in 1965 at the age of 50. Matthews had played nearly 700 times for Stoke City and Blackpool, and 84 times for England and did not receive a single booking (warning for bad behaviour) in his entire career.

Sir Malcolm Campbell (1885–1948)

World land and water speed record holder. Campbell started racing motorbikes in his teens and later moved on to cars. From 1912, he called his racing car *Blue Bird* and painted it blue. His land speed record cars and water speed record boats would be called *Blue Bird* too. He set his first official land speed record of 235 kph (146 mph) in 1924.

After he had broken the land speed record for the fifth time, in 1931, he was knighted. He set the last of his nine land speed records in 1935, when he was the first person to drive a car faster than 300 mph (485 kph). Next, he turned his attention to the water speed record. He broke it, with a speed of 203 kph (126 mph) in 1937. He broke it another three times by 1939, raising the record to 228 kph (141 mph).

Malcolm Campbell's son, Donald (1921–1967), carried on in his father's footsteps. His boats and cars were called *Bluebird*. He set one land speed record and seven water speed records (more than anyone else) between 1955 and 1964. In 1964, he became the first and only person ever to break the land and water speed records in the same year. He died while trying to break the water speed record again. Donald Campbell's daughter Gina (b.1946) is a record breaker too. She set women's water speed records in 1984 and 1990. Malcolm Campbell's nephew, Don Wales (b1960), has also set speed records in electric cars.

Mr Whoppit

Donald Campbell was very superstitious. He carried a lucky mascot with him on his record attempts – a teddy bear called Mr Whoppit. It was recovered after his fatal crash in 1967 and his daughter Gina carried it on her record attempts.

The most famous British land speed record holders

J.G. Parry-Thomas: 1926
272 kph (169 mph) Babs

Sir Malcolm Campbell: 1924, 25, 27, 28, 31, 32, 35
484 kph (301 mph) Campbell-Railton Blue Bird

John Cobb: 1938, 39, 47
630 kph (394 mph) Railton

Donald Campbell: 1964
648 kph (403 mph) Bluebird-Proteus CN7

Richard Noble: 1983
1020 kph (634 mph) Thrust 2

Andy Green: 1997
1227 kph (763 mph) Thrust SSC

Thrust SSC
(SuperSonic
Car) is a British
jet-propelled car
developed by
Richard Noble,
Glynne Bowsher,
Ron Ayers and
Jeremy Bliss.

153

Sir Jack Hobbs (1882–1963)

Renowned cricketer. Hobbs scored more runs (61,237) and more centuries (197) in first-class cricket than anyone else. His professional cricket career began with Surrey in 1905. W.G. Grace played in the same match and said of Hobbs, *'He's going to be a good 'un'*. His cricket career was interrupted by World War I, in which he served in the Royal Flying Corps. In 1928–9, at the age of 46, he became the oldest man ever to score a century in a Test match. He was so highly respected by other players that he was nicknamed The Master. He was the first professional cricketer to be knighted.

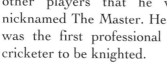

Sir Stirling Moss (b.1929)

The greatest racing driver never to win the Grand Prix World Championship. Motor-racing was in the Moss family as both of his parents took part in motor-races and rallies. Stirling Moss learned to drive at the age of nine! During his racing career, between 1948 and 1962, he entered 529 races and won 212 of them, including 16 Formula 1 Grands Prix. He came second in the World Championship four times, but never won. In 1962, he was badly hurt in an accident on the Goodwood circuit and was in a coma for a month. When he recovered, he retired from top-level motor-racing, although he continued to race historic cars.

Roger Bannister (b.1929)

The first person to run a mile in less than 4 minutes. After a disappointing performance at the 1952 Olympics, Bannister set himself the goal of running a mile in under 4 minutes for the first time in history. On May 6, 1954, in Oxford, he began a carefully planned race. Chris Brasher (later a co-founder of the London Marathon) and Christopher Chataway ran as pacemakers for Bannister, who collapsed exhausted as he crossed the finish line. Bannister's time was 3 minutes and 59.4 seconds. He had run the mile faster than anyone before and broken the 4-minute barrier. Later the same year, he retired from athletics to pursue a career in medicine.

Sir Jackie Stewart (b.1939)

World Champion racing driver known as *'The Flying Scot'*. Stewart was working as a car mechanic when he was offered the chance to test-drive racing cars. He was such a good driver that he was soon racing, winning and working his way up through Formula 3 and 2 to the pinnacle of the sport – Formula 1.

Between 1965 and 1973, he won 27 Formula 1 races, which was a record at that time. After an accident in 1966, which he was lucky to survive, he became a tireless campaigner for better safety standards, emergency services and medical care in motor-racing. He won three Formula 1 World Championships, in 1969, 71 and 73, and retired in 1973. He returned in 1997 to run his own Formula 1 team with his son, Paul.

British Formula One Champions

Driver	World Champion in
Mike Hawthorn (1929–1959)	1958
Graham Hill (1929–1975)	1962, 1968
Jim Clark (1936–1968)	1963, 1965
John Surtees (b.1934)	1964
Jackie Stewart (b.1939)	1969, 1971, 1973
James Hunt (1947–1993)	1976
Nigel Mansell (b.1953)	1992
Damon Hill (b.1960)	1996
Lewis Hamilton (b.1985)	2008
Jenson Button (b.1980)	2009

John Surtees is the only person to win world championships on both two wheels and four, having won six motorcycle world championships before winning the Formula 1 title.

Bobby Moore (1941–1993)

The greatest captain of the greatest England football team. Moore joined West Ham as a youth player in 1956 and made his professional appearance against Manchester United two years later. He made more than 500 appearances for West Ham and captained them for more than 10 years. Moore was selected for the England under-23 squad in 1960 and progressed to the full England squad two years later, where he was named captain in 1963.

Moore played for England 108 times and captained them 90 times. The team's greatest achievement was its victory against Germany in the 1966 World Cup final under the management of Alf Ramsey (1920–1999). Ramsey was knighted the following year. In 1974, Moore moved to Fulham for three years. After a short spell playing in the USA, he retired as a player in 1978. He had a short but unsuccessful time as a manager and died in 1993 after a two-year battle against cancer.

The 1966 World Cup winning team

1	Gordon Banks	Goalkeeper
2	George Cohen	Right back
5	Jack Charlton	Centre back
6	Bobby Moore (Captain)	Centre back
3	Ray Wilson	Left back
4	Nobby Stiles	Midfielder
7	Alan Ball	Midfielder
9	Bobby Charlton	Midfielder
16	Martin Peters	Midfielder
10	Geoff Hurst	Centreforward
21	Roger Hunt	Centreforward

Manager: Alf Ramsey

George Best (1946–2005)

One of the most talented football players of his generation. George Best was born in Belfast and was discovered by a scout for Manchester United at the age of only 15. The scout's telegram to the manager, Matt Busby, simply said, *'I've found you a genius'*. Best's speed, balance, ability to use either foot and pop star looks made him a favourite with fans. He was named European Footballer of the Year in 1968 and stayed with United until 1974. He also played for Northern Ireland 37 times. However, he became increasingly distracted by his superstar lifestyle. He opened his own nightclubs and fashion boutiques, and his focus drifted from football. He played for a number of clubs in South Africa, Ireland, the USA, Scotland, Australia and England over the next 10 years. Eventually, years of heavy drinking took its toll on his health. He had a liver transplant in 2002, but continued drinking and died in 2005 at the age of only 59.

Daley Thompson (b.1958)

The greatest decathlete. Daley Thompson won decathlon gold medals at the 1980 and 1984 Olympic Games, and broke the world record for the event four times. He also won three Commonwealth titles along with World and European Championships. He dominated the event until a hamstring injury forced him to retire in 1992. To many people, he is the world's greatest ever all-round athlete.

The decathlon

The decathlon is an athletic competition comprising ten track and field events – the shot put, discus, javelin, long jump, high jump, pole vault, 100 metres, 400 metres, 1500 metres and 110 metres hurdles. The competitors are awarded points according to how well they do in each event and the winner is the athlete with the most points.

Linford Christie (b.1960)

Britain's greatest 100 metres sprinter. The 100 metres sprint is one of the most fiercely competitive of all athletic events. Christie won the 100 metres gold medal at the 1986 and 1990 European Championships, the 1992 Olympic Games and the 1993 World Championships. He was the first British or European athlete ever to run the 100 metres in under 10 seconds, in 1988. In 1993, he was the first track athlete ever to hold the European, Commonwealth, World, and Olympic titles at the same time. During his career, he won a total of 23 major championship medals, including 10 gold. He was captain of the British Athletic Team from 1995 to 1997. When he retired in 1997, he was Britain's most successful athlete.

Outstanding British sports men and women

Fred Perry (1909–1995) World number one tennis player in the 1930s. He won the men's singles championship at Wimbledon three times.

Lester Piggott (b.1935) 11 times Champion Jockey who rode 4,493 winners.

Virginia Wade (b.1945) Won the women's singles championship at Wimbledon in 1977.

Steve Ovett (b.1955) Won the 800 m gold medal at the Moscow Olympics in 1980 and set world records at 1500 metres and the mile.

Sebastian Coe (b.1956) Won the 1500 m gold medal at the Moscow Olympics in 1980 and set 11 world records. He became a politician and led the successful bid for the 2012 Olympics in London. He was created Baron Coe in 2000.

Tessa Sanderson (b.1956) Javelin thrower, competed at six Olympic Games from 1976 to 1996 and won gold at the Los Angeles Olympics in 1984.

Frank Bruno (b.1961) WBC heavyweight boxing champion in 1996.

Sir Steve Redgrave (b.1962) Won rowing gold medals at five consecutive Olympic Games (1984–2000).

Lennox Lewis (b.1965) Undisputed world champion heavyweight boxer in 1999.

Dame Kelly Holmes (b.1970) Middle distance runner, won gold at 800 m and 1500 m at the 2004 Olympic Games.

Torvill (b.1957) and Dean (b.1958) British, European, World and Olympic figure skating champions.

26 million Britons watched Torvill and Dean record the first ever perfect score with their performance of Bolero in the 1984 Olympics.

CHAPTER ELEVEN

MISCELLANEOUS

S ome Britons do not fit neatly into categories. They include evangelists, nurses, social reformers, entrepreneurs and the unique Diana, Princess of Wales. Their contributions to British life and history are wonderfully varied, as are their fates. Some lived out their days in peace, whereas others came to a violent end. Some acquired great wealth, while others had hardly a penny to their name.

Sir Christopher Wren
(1632–1723)

Architect of St Paul's Cathedral in London. Wren showed an early talent for maths and science. He became a professor of astronomy and was a founding member of the Royal Society, the world's oldest learned society for the promotion of scientific knowledge. His interest in science and engineering led him to study architecture.

After the Great Fire of London, he was appointed the king's Surveyor of Works, which placed him in control of all government building. He was responsible for rebuilding 51 churches as well as St Paul's Cathedral, a mammoth project that took 36 years to complete. The many other buildings he designed include the Royal Observatory, Greenwich, and Trinity College Library in Cambridge. Wren was knighted in 1673. When he died, he was buried in St Paul's Cathedral. His gravestone says, in Latin, *'Reader, if you seek his memorial, look around you'*.

The dome on top of the cathedral is a very clever design. It looks like a simple stone dome, but it is actually three domes – an inner dome made of brick and an outer dome made of wood with a brick cone between the two. It was a brilliant way to combine enormous size with minimal weight.

St Paul's Cathedral is home to the memorials of Alexander Fleming, T.E. Lawrence, Florence Nightingale, Henry Moore and many more.

John Wesley (1703–1791)

Cleric and religious thinker who founded the Methodist Church. Wesley was deeply religious from an early age and devoted his life to preaching Christianity. In 1735, he went to the American colony of Georgia for two years, but the high-church views he held then were not popular. On his return to England, he turned to the Moravians, a European Protestant Church, for help. He was deeply affected by them. He travelled the country preaching to anyone who would listen to him. Following an unconventional path like this was very difficult in Wesley's time, but even so, he attracted followers, who became known as Methodists. By the time of his death, the Methodist movement had more than 76,000 members. Wesley once said, '*I look upon the whole world as my parish.*' Today, there are 70 million Methodists in 'the whole world'.

Elizabeth Fry (1780–1845)

Prison reformer. Elizabeth Fry was born into a Quaker family in Norfolk. Even in her teens, she was concerned for the poor, the sick and prisoners. She collected clothes for the poor and visited sick people in her neighbourhood.

When she visited Newgate Prison in London, she was horrified by its filthy conditions. She brought food and clothes into the prison for the inmates. She visited other prisons and formed local societies to press for improved conditions for prisoners.

Fry also helped the homeless. After she saw the body of a homeless boy who had frozen to death in a London street, she started a night shelter for the homeless, and also arranged for volunteers to visit the homes of the poor. In 1840, she opened a training school for nurses. Some of Fry's nurses accompanied Florence Nightingale to look after British soldiers during the Crimean War.

Mary Seacole (1805–1881)
A nurse whose reputation rivalled that of Florence Nightingale. Mary Seacole was born in Jamaica. She learned Creole medicine and nursing skills at her mother's boarding house, where British soldiers and sailors stayed. When she heard of the poor medical facilities for British soldiers fighting in the Crimean War in 1854, she travelled to London and asked to be sent to the Crimea as a nurse. Her

request was turned down, but she went anyway. She established a British Hotel where she served meals and looked after casualties from the battlefield, sometimes coming under fire herself. She returned to England after the war, penniless and in bad health. When her sorry state was reported in newspapers, a fund was set up to support her in 1857. Her autobiography, *Wonderful Adventures of Mrs Seacole*, was published in the same year.

Thomas Cook (1808–1892)

The founder of popular tourism. Cook was an enthusiastic supporter of the temperance (anti-alcohol) movement. He arranged his first excursion in 1841 to take temperance campaigners on the 18 km (11 mile) journey from Leicester to Loughborough for a rally. The one shilling

that each person paid for the return journey included their rail fare and food. Cook arranged journeys for pleasure as well as for the temperance movement. Then the Midland Counties Railway Company made a permanent arrangement with him for more excursions, so he started a business to manage them. And the journeys went further afield.

In the early 1860s, he started arranging trips and tours to the continent, and in 1865 he started tours to the United States. In 1879, management of the company passed to Cook's son, John, and Cook retired to Leicestershire. By 1888 the company had established offices around the world.

A trip to Brighton's pleasure beach and Palace Pier was a popular holiday activity for Britain's wealthier classes.

florence Nightingale
(1820-1910)

Nurse who was known as *'The Lady With the Lamp'*. Nightingale decided to become a nurse in 1844, despite opposition from her family. They eventually gave in to her wishes and she went to Germany in 1851 to train as a nurse. Two years later, she was working as a hospital superintendent in Harley Street, London.

In 1854, she heard about the poor medical facilities for wounded British soldiers during the Crimean War – a war between Russia and allied countries including Britain. At the request of the war minister, she led a group of 38 nurses to Turkey. When she arrived in Scutari, she found soldiers dying from infections in filthy conditions. More soldiers died of infections such as typhoid and cholera than died of their wounds. While Nightingale and her nurses improved medical care and nutrition, a Sanitary Commission sent from Britain improved hygiene standards. The death rate fell. Nightingale got her nickname, *'The Lady with the Lamp'*, at this time, because she toured the wards every night, lighting her way with a lamp.

In 1860, after her return to England, she started a training school for nurses at St Thomas's Hospital, London. She also advised the government on nursing and public health.

When Florence Nightingale was working in Scutari, the way infectious diseases spread was not understood. The miasma theory of infection was widely believed at the time. Miasma is smelly, unpleasant air, which was thought to contain poisonous fumes that caused disease. A series of discoveries and experiments in the second half of the nineteenth century showed that the miasma theory was false and it was replaced by the germ theory of infection.

International Nurses Day is celebrated on Florence Nightingale's birthday – May 12.

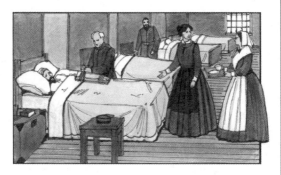

Florence Nightingale's voice was saved for posterity in a phonograph recording from 1890 and preserved in the British Library Sound Archive.

William Booth (1829–1912)
Founder of the Salvation Army. A committed Christian since his teens, Booth joined the Methodist Church and became a minister. He felt the need to do more to take the word of God to ordinary people. He resigned as a minister and formed his own movement called The Christian Mission. His work was not popular with everyone and stones were often thrown at him. In 1878, he changed the movement's name to The Salvation Army. The new name and Booth's fiery sermons attracted more and more followers. Its members wore uniform, had ranks and followed their own flag. Unlike other church organisations, The Salvation Army allowed women to preach and hold senior positions. During Booth's lifetime, The Salvation Army spread to 58 countries and colonies.

Edith Cavell (1865–1915)

British nurse executed during World War I. After working as a governess, Edith Cavell trained as a nurse. In 1907, she went to work in Belgium. When German troops over-ran Belgium, she treated anyone who needed help, whatever their nationality. She also hid British soldiers and helped them to get to neutral Holland. She enabled about 200 soldiers to escape. She was arrested in 1915 and tried by a military court for breaking German military law by helping enemies of the German people. She was found guilty and sentenced to death. Despite protests, she was executed by firing squad on October 12, 1915. Her execution was widely used for propaganda purposes by Britain and the USA, who portrayed it as an act of savagery by an uncivilised enemy. After the war, her body was returned to England and buried next to Norwich Cathedral.

Emmeline Pankhurst
(1858-1928)

Campaigner for women's voting rights. When Pankhurst was growing up, women in Britain were not allowed to vote in general (national) elections. A number of organisations were formed to campaign for suffrage (voting rights) for women. The people who joined them and supported them were generally known as suffragists.

Pankhurst founded one of these organisations, the Women's Franchise League, in 1889. In 1903, she helped to form the Women's Social and Political Union (WSPU). Its members, who were known as suffragettes, were often arrested for taking part in demonstrations, smashing windows and disrupting public meetings. Some went on hunger strike in prison and were force-fed. When World War I began, they ceased their activities and joined the war effort. In 1918, limited voting rights were granted to some women. In 1928, women were finally given the same voting rights as men. Pankhurst died a few weeks later.

Death Dive

In 1913, suffragette Emily Davison (1872-1913) ran out in front of the King's horse and died a few days later. A note calling for votes for women was found pinned to her clothes. Was she mad, or a heroine? Or was her death a tragic accident? People could not agree.

Sir Richard Branson (b.1950)

One of Britain's most successful businessmen and one of the world's richest people. Richard Branson is best known for his Virgin Group of about 200 companies in more than 30 countries and for his daredevil record attempts. Branson had his first business successes in his teens and twenties, publishing a magazine and founding a mail order record company called Virgin. He went on to set up the Virgin Megastore record shops. In the 1980s, he expanded his business interests, notably by setting up Virgin Atlantic Airways. In the 1990s, he started Virgin Railways. In 2004, he started a space tourism company, Virgin Galactic, to take tourists on brief flights into space. The records and 'firsts' he has achieved include the fastest crossing of the Atlantic Ocean by boat, the first crossing of the Atlantic Ocean by hot-air balloon, the fastest crossing of the Pacific Ocean by hot-air balloon, and the fastest crossing of the English Channel in an amphibious vehicle.

Richard Branson does not wear business suits and very rarely wears a tie.

Diana, Princess of Wales (1961–1997)

Diana Spencer was the youngest daughter of the Viscount and Viscountess of Althorp. After leaving school, she worked as a nanny and kindergarten assistant in London. She attracted press interest when rumours of a relationship with Prince Charles, the Prince of Wales, began circulating. Their engagement was announced on February 24, 1981. They were married at St Paul's cathedral on July 29 of the same year. More than half a million people lined the streets to see them and 750 million more watched on television.

Diana quickly became a favourite with the public. In 1982, she gave birth to Prince William and, in 1984, Prince Henry – known as Harry. Like other members of the royal family, Diana undertook charity work. Her work with AIDS charities received a lot of attention. Later, she gave public support to a campaign to ban landmines. By 1987, her marriage was known to be in trouble. She had also been suffering from the eating disorder bulimia. She separated from Prince Charles in 1992 and divorce followed in 1996.

The next year she was photographed with Dodi Fayed, son of Mohamed Al Fayed, the then owner of Harrods. On August 30, 1997, the couple set out by car from the Ritz Hotel in Paris with photographers in hot pursuit. As their car entered an underpass, the driver lost control and hit a concrete pillar. The driver and Dodi Fayed were killed instantly. A bodyguard, Trevor Rees-Jones, survived, although seriously injured. Diana survived the crash but died soon afterwards in the early hours of August 31. An estimated 2.5 billion people worldwide watched the broadcast of her funeral. She was buried on an island in the middle of a lake at her family's estate at Althorp.

Top Row (L-R): Charles Dickens, David Lloyd George, Nelson, Jane Austen, Florence Nightingale
Second Row (L-R): Salman Rushdie, Lord Byron, Elizabeth Fry, Frank Bruno, Princess Diana, Daley Thompson, Isambard Kingdom Brunel
Third Row (L-R): The Beatles, William Shakespeare, Noor Inayat Khan
Fourth Row (L-R): Henry VIII, Margaret Thatcher, Robert Burns, Duke of Wellington, Mary Shelley, Queen Victoria
Bottom Row (L-R): Winston Churchill, Boudicca

181

Glossary

artificial intelligence The intelligence of machines such as computers and robots.

Big Bang The explosion of energy that is said to have been the origin of the universe.

black hole A massive object formed when a giant star explodes, with gravity so powerful that even light cannot escape from it.

Britannia An ancient name for Britain and also the personification of Britain, usually a helmeted woman carrying a shield and trident.

British Empire The United Kingdom and the territories it governed, which encompassed more than a quarter of the world's population and more than a quarter of the world's land surface at the end of World War I.

cosmologist A scientist who studies the origin and development of the Universe.

DNA Deoxyribonucleic acid, the substance in a living cell that contains the instructions necessary for the growth and functioning of an organism.

Emmy An award given for outstanding television programmes and performances.

Flemish From a region called Flanders, divided between France, Belgium and The Netherlands.

geostationary orbit An orbit 36,000 km above the Earth's equator, in which satellites go round the Earth once a day and so stay in the same spot in the sky.

Grammy An award given for achievements in the recording industry.

GLOSSARY

hung, drawn and quartered A savage method of execution in which the victim is hung, then cut down while still alive, disembowelled, then beheaded and cut into four quarters.

locomotive A vehicle for pulling trains.

monarch A king, queen or emperor.

National Theatre A publicly funded theatre company based on the South Bank of the River Thames in London.

navigable river A river big enough for boats or ships.

Oscar The Academy Award given for excellence in film-making and screen acting.

patent An official document that recognises someone as the inventor of something and gives them the sole right to make, use or sell it.

PhD Doctor of Philosophy, the highest level of degree, above Bachelor's and Master's degrees.

Poet Laureate A poet appointed by the Queen to write poems about important occasions.

Puritans A group of extreme Protestants in the sixteenth and seventeenth centuries.

Quaker A member of a Christian movement called the Religious Society of Friends.

shell shock A psychological condition caused by the stress of military combat.

sonnet A poem 14 lines long with a formal rhyme structure.

spiritualist Religious belief that involves communication with the spirits of dead people.

state funeral A public funeral arranged for an important person.

virologist A scientist who studies viruses.

Timeline

950,000 BCE The first humans reach Britain.

33,000 BCE Our species, homo sapiens, arrives in Britain.

8,000 BCE The ice begins to retreat from Britain at the end of the last ice age.

6,000 BCE The sea cuts off Britain from Europe.

43 The Romans invade Britain.

303 The man who will become known as St George, the patron saint of England, is executed by the Roman Emperor Diocletian.

1415 King Henry V is victorious against the French at the Battle of Agincourt.

1535 Sir Thomas More is executed.

1580 Sir Francis Drake becomes the first Englishman to sail around the world.

1588 The Spanish Armada attacks the English fleet.

1649 King Charles I is executed.

1653 Oliver Cromwell makes himself Lord Protector of England.

1660 The monarchy is restored with the coronation of King Charles II.

1666 The Great Fire of London.

1707 Great Britain becomes a single nation when England and Wales are united with Scotland.

1712 Thomas Newcomen invents the steam engine.

1755 Samuel Johnson's *Dictionary of the English Language* is published.

1796 Captain James Cook commands a voyage to observe the transit of Venus across the Sun. Edward Jenner successfully tests a vaccine for smallpox.

Timeline

1804 Richard Trevithick builds the first steam railway locomotive.

1805 Horatio Nelson is victorious at the Battle of Trafalgar.

1815 Emperor Napoleon is defeated by the Duke of Wellington's forces at the Battle of Waterloo.

1818 Mary Shelley's novel, *Frankenstein*, is published.

1829 The Stephenson locomotive *Rocket* wins the Rainhill Trials.

1831 Charles Darwin sets out on a five-year scientific expedition on-board *HMS Beagle*.

1843 Isambard Kingdom Brunel's tunnel under the River Thames opens.

1845 Sir John Franklin's expedition vanishes while searching for the North West Passage.

1854 Florence Nightingale goes to Scutari to look after British soldiers.

1859 Charles Darwin's book, *The Origin of Species*, is published.

1876 Alexander Graham Bell invents the telephone.

1878 The Salvation Army is formed by William Booth.

1887 *A Study in Scarlet*, the first Sherlock Holmes story by Sir Arthur Conan Doyle, is published.

1897 Queen Victoria's diamond jubilee is celebrated.

1901 The rule of Queen Victoria, Britain's longest reigning monarch, comes to an end.

1912 Robert Falcon Scott dies while attempting to be the first to reach the South Pole.

1914 World War I begins.

1915 Nurse Edith Cavell is executed for helping allied soldiers to escape from Belgium.

1917 Lawrence of Arabia and his Arab fighters take the port of Aqaba.

1918 World War I ends.

1921 Ireland is partitioned, forming the Republic of Ireland and Northern Ireland.

1924 John Logie Baird invents television.

1928 Women are granted equal voting rights. Alexander Fleming discovers the antibiotic effect of penicillin.

1930 Frank Whittle invents the jet engine. Amy Johnson becomes the first woman to fly solo from Britain to Australia. Sir Malcolm Campbell sets the last of his nine land speed records.

1939 World War II begins.

1941 Record-breaking pilot Amy Johnson dies after crashing into the sea.

1942 Lt-General Montgomery's Eighth Army is victorious at the Battle of El Alamein in Egypt. Vera Lynn records 'We'll Meet Again'.

1945 Arthur C. Clarke suggests placing satellites in geostationary orbit for communications. World War II ends.

1947 India gains its independence from Britain.

1948 The artist and sculptor, Henry Moore, wins the prestigious Venice Biennale.

1953 Francis Crick and James Watson discover the structure of DNA.

1954 Roger Bannister runs the world's first sub four minute mile.

1956 Christopher Cockerell invents the hovercraft.

1957 Patrick Moore presents the first edition of *The Sky at Night* on television.

1964 Donald Campbell becomes the first, and only, person to set a world land speed record and world water speed record in the same year.

Timeline

1966 The England football team, under the captaincy of Bobby Moore, wins the World Cup.

1967 Jocelyn Bell Burnell discovers the first pulsar. Francis Chichester completes a single-handed round-the-world voyage.

1969 Robin Knox-Johnston completes the first single-handed non-stop round-the-world voyage. Wally Herbert becomes the first man to walk to the North Pole.

1970 The Beatles split up.

1973 Jackie Stewart wins the last of his three world driver's championships.

1979 Margaret Thatcher becomes Britain's first woman Prime Minister. Earl Mountbatten of Burma is murdered by the IRA.

1980 Ex-Beatle John Lennon is murdered in New York.

1984 Alex Jeffreys invents genetic profiling.

1988 A murderer is identified by means of genetic profiling for the first time.

1989 The site of Shakespeare's Globe Theatre is discovered in London.

1991 The World Wide Web, invented by Tim Berners-Lee, is made available to the public.

1993 The Salariya Book Company moves into Book House.

1994 Britain is re-connected with Europe for the first time in 8,000 years by the Channel Tunnel under the English Channel.

1997 Andy Green sets the first supersonic land speed record. Diana, Princess of Wales, dies in a car accident in Paris.

2009 Mike Perham becomes the youngest round-the-world sailor at the age of 17.

Index

Very Peculiar Histories™

Ancient Egypt
Mummy Myth and Magic
Jim Pipe
ISBN: 978-1-906714-92-5

The Blitz
David Arscott
ISBN: 978-1-907184-18-5

Brighton
David Arscott
ISBN: 978-1-906714-89-5

Castles
Jacqueline Morley
ISBN: 978-1-907184-48-2

Christmas
Fiona Macdonald
ISBN: 978-1-907184-50-5

Global Warming
Ian Graham
ISBN: 978-1-907184-51-2

Tudors
Jim Pipe
ISBN: 978-1-907184-58-1

Ireland
Jim Pipe
ISBN: 978-1-905638-98-7

London
Jim Pipe
ISBN: 978-1-907184-26-0

Rations
David Arscott
ISBN: 978-1-907184-25-3

Scotland
Fiona Macdonald

Vol. 1: From ancient times
to Robert the Bruce
ISBN: 978-1-906370-91-6

Vol. 2: From the Stewarts
to modern Scotland
ISBN: 978-1-906714-79-6

Vampires
Fiona Macdonald
ISBN: 978-1-907184-39-0

Victorian Servants
Fiona Macdonald
ISBN: 978-1-907184-49-9

Wales
Rupert Matthews
ISBN: 978-1-907184-19-2

Yorkshire
John Malam
ISBN: 978-1-907184-57-4

Heroes, Gods and Monsters of
Ancient Greek Mythology
Michael Ford
ISBN: 978-1-906370-92-3

Heroes, Gods and Monsters of
Celtic Mythology
Fiona Macdonald
ISBN: 978-1-905638-97-0